THE CANDIDATE

For F and M, wherever you are

hope it helps
you to make
it to Dáil eireann!
SOKeffe.

THE CANDIDATE

SUSAN O'KEEFFE

CURRACH
PRESS

First published in 2009 by

CURRACH PRESS

55A Spruce Avenue, Stillorgan Industrial Park, Blackrock, County Dublin

www.currach.ie

1 3 5 4 2

Cover by bluett

Origination by Currach Press

Printed in Ireland by ColourBooks, Baldoyle Industrial Estate, Dublin 13

ISBN: 978-1-85607-990-7

Acknowledgements

Thank you:

To all the people who voted for me

To those who canvassed for me

To those who funded the campaign

To the other candidates

To the *Irish Daily Mail* for use of articles

To tea-makers across the North-West

To those who quietly kept the balls in the air

To those who helped anonymously; in this book I use their initials

To David, Kirsten, Cormac and Pat who kept going

To Neil Ward for smiling

To Paul Daly for his calmness

To Michael D and Sabina for their warmth and encouragement

To Eamon for his leadership

To my friends who kept me sane

To Mags for everything

To the Labour Party for its faith

To my family for their patience and love

Contents

Foreword by Eamon Gilmore TD, Leader of the Labour Party

From the day I became leader of the Labour Party in September 2007, I was apprehensive about the 2009 local and European elections. These elections would be my first electoral test as leader. Labour had done very well in the previous local elections, breaking the hundred-seat barrier for the first time. It would be hard to repeat this. Our only European seat was in Dublin and that constituency was being reduced from a four-seater to a three-seater. Labour had not won Munster or Leinster for thirty years.

By the beginning of 2009, we had selected Alan Kelly and Nessa Childers to contest Ireland South and Ireland East respectively. Proinsias de Rossa had announced his intention of standing for re-election in Dublin. And that left Ireland North-West – Labour's weakest European constituency. Some counselled not contesting it at all and concentrating our limited resources on the three constituencies where we had some realistic prospect of winning. I was privately determined that Labour should have candidates everywhere. Every voter should have the opportunity to vote Labour in the European elections. And since I hail from Galway myself I was loath for Labour to abandon the west!

But who would stand? There were no volunteers! A prospective Dáil candidate perhaps? Or somebody completely new who might help to broaden Labour's appeal? Jan O'Sullivan, the party's health spokesperson, had picked up on the grapevine that Susan O'Keeffe might be interested. I did not know her personally but she ticked a lot of boxes. She was living in Sligo. She had built a strong reputation as a journalist. She knew about the rural economy. She could help to widen Labour's electorate. She had shown remarkable courage during the Beef Tribunal and courage was a quality that would be needed by a Labour candidate in Connacht and Ulster!

First there was a lot of talking to be done. Was Susan interested? How would it impact on her own career? What did she think of Labour's approach to certain issues, particularly issues related to Europe? What kind of campaign could we mount? How would we resource it? Could she switch hats from being a journalist to being a politician?

Susan and I met in Leinster House to talk through all this. She remarked, as our paths crossed at the door of LH2000, that the last time she had been around the Dáil was back in the early 1990s, when she spoke to the then Labour Party leader Dick Spring about the beef industry. I know conversations continued between Susan and party colleagues about how a campaign might work and whether it was feasible in such a short space of time.

I was delighted when Susan joined the Labour Party and agreed to be the party's European candidate in our most challenging constituency. We made the announcement to the press on the eve of Labour's annual conference in Mullingar. It was the end of March and the elections were just two months away!

Susan was a great candidate. She threw herself into the campaign, crisscrossing a constituency that stretched from the suburbs of Limerick to the borders of County Louth and County Meath. The switch from journalist to candidate, interviewer to interviewee cannot have been easy but within a couple of weeks, Susan was responding like a veteran politician, while displaying the novelty and freshness that can come only from somebody new to politics.

Only those of us who have stood for election fully understand how vulnerable and exposed a candidate can feel. At times it is terrifying. Susan showed remarkable fortitude, as she campaigned in places where there was little Labour presence, came to terms with sometimes disappointing opinion polls and jostled for attention with the other candidates.

No commentator gave Susan even the remotest chance of winning a seat. This was a huge handicap, because Declan Ganley's candidacy meant that many voters faced the choice of voting for Ganley as the 'anti-establishment' candidate or voting for a potential winner to stop Ganley, the 'anti-European'.

For Susan to get 30,000 votes in such a contest was truly remarkable. It was a tribute to her own qualities as a candidate and to the extent to which she impressed the voters she met. It was also due to the hard work of the Labour organisation throughout the constituency and the small team of volunteers, led by Mags Murphy, who organised the campaign.

Susan didn't win a seat but for me, her 30,000 votes was a sweeter success than the three European seats we won in the other three constituencies. At last, Labour has an electoral base across the west of Ireland and the border areas. We can build on the foundations laid by Susan O'Keeffe.

The Labour Party – and politics generally – needs more new

candidates like Susan O'Keeffe: people with courage, integrity, new ideas and fresh appeal.

I am glad she has written a book about her experience, because in these cynical times, politics also need participants who can describe and communicate, openly and honestly, what politics are really like.

INTRODUCTION

Can you be looking in one day and looking out the next? Outside, then inside – and so quickly. So it was. For my entire journalistic career, I have essentially been on the outside looking in, trying to see the wrongs, the failings, the greed, the lies and the mistakes. Rarely have I dealt with happy success stories – there were a few but as the years passed, fewer, as I concentrated my efforts on trying to draw attention to injustice.

Over the years, people had suggested, sometimes as a joke, that I should go into politics. I had considered it on and off but it never seemed like the right moment. The children were young, the work I was doing exciting and the 'right' opportunity never seemed to present itself. Living in the UK, politics felt remote and unconnected to the real world, especially with the firmly entrenched concept of the 'safe seat'.

Now in Mullingar, County Westmeath, on 27 March 2009, I crossed the line to the other side. I was visibly on the 'other side' of the press conference, as Labour Party leader Eamon Gilmore and party president Michael D Higgins welcomed me to the party and praised my decision to stand as a candidate in the European elections. The lights were shining on me and I was answering the questions, most of which, I can honestly say, I struggle to recall now, so surreal was the sense of switching sides. Emotionally I had crossed the line, as I recognised most of the journalists with whom I would once have stood or sat: now suddenly they seemed a long way away from where I was standing, as I tried hard to smile and wondered where all this might lead.

I remembered the wrong side from once before. The day my trial (for not revealing my sources to the Beef Tribunal) ended, on 25 January 1995, I was asked to appear on that evening's *Late Late Show*, then hosted by Gay Byrne. As I walked through the back of the studio from the green room, I found myself at the top of the stairs which led to Gay's set. In a split second, I had the feeling that I had somehow got up from my seat at home and walked through the television and into the set! So striking was the thought that I had to stop myself stumbling; the replay would show a slight pause on one step. Like millions of others in Ireland I had spent an entire lifetime watching the scene play out week after week as guest after guest walked down the stairs: finding myself on the step was to be on the wrong side.

The difference was that, in Mullingar, I knew the moment would last longer than that. I had made not one but two decisions. One was to stop looking in, looking for mistakes, errors or incompetence. The second was that I would aim to replace the talking and the telling with doing. I was switching sides to stand up and do something, rather than watch others doing it and comment on their failings. The truth is that I wasn't sure I could achieve that but I certainly felt it was right to try.

There was one finite thing I could aim for that I believed was worth doing: that was to do my bit to ensure that Declan Ganley was not elected. On the face of it, his politics and mine are utterly opposed and my inclusion on the ballot paper could hardly, in theory, have an impact on the voters he hoped to entice. Except that, in practice, there is always confusion among voters and that sends some votes astray. (Indeed the count proved this: some of my Number Twos were given to Ganley and some of his Twos were given to me!) My involvement meant I could oppose him directly, wherever and whenever I could. Finally, by running I was very simply increasing the choice for all voters, especially those who wished to vote against the government.

Many people have asked me why I bothered, when all the figures, the history and the tradition made clear even before the start of the campaign that the Labour Party was unlikely to win a seat, especially coming so late to the game with all three incumbents standing again. (Fianna Fáil's Seán Ó Neachtain did not pull out until 20 April.) I knew the figures and I guessed that whatever way you chewed them up and spat them out, they would fall in a pretty similar pattern. But sometimes you have to make decisions which are not based solely on the cold, hard facts and this felt like one of those moments.

There was something else: the profound changes in our society as a result of the recession and the government's slow and stumbling response to that. I found that I was able to criticise what they were doing or failing to do and join with others in this necessary activity. But I began to think that I should try to be more positive, to do things rather than to talk about other people failing to do things. So if I went and 'stood somewhere else in the room', it might enable me to have an input and to contribute in a different way. All I hoped was that I could make some contribution from this side of the line. Oh – and not fall flat on my face!

How It All Began

My political career started in a thatched pub in Ballisodare, County Sligo. O'Connor's Pub advertises having 'the best barman in Sligo', but I wasn't paying much attention to that. This, after all, was the first official meeting between the party and me to discuss whether I should stand in the European elections. How Irish to end up in a pub – even if both of us are drinking water! But that's where I meet Mark Garrett, Eamon Gilmore's chief adviser. We get on well: we chat about the short time-frame, about the other candidates, about the size of the constituency and about Labour's prospects. He seems keen but doesn't press me or try to persuade me. Neither do I feel he is trying to trick me or convince me of anything. It's an open and honest exchange.

I leave the meeting confused because now I have stepped off the edge – a baby step, yes, but a step. I have never been a member of a political party and here I find myself not simply filling in a form but possible standing as a candidate – without ever having been in the party!

Of course it's not quite the first conversation and it's not the last. There are a few trips to Leinster House, a meeting with Eamon Gilmore, quite a few phone calls and emails as I think of more and more questions and need more and more answers. And there's a long round of conversations with friends. Most think it's a good idea. The children wonder why I didn't do it before. Some ask obvious questions like: will I win? Others ask practical questions like: how will we live if I am not working? Sometimes I don't like practical questions but these are the moments that make me realise I will probably go ahead and do it. I have quite a history of what those self-improvement books call 'following your instinct' but what I describe as 'jumping off the cliff'. I can spend ten minutes choosing between two brands of ice cream but life decisions rarely take me more than ten seconds. It doesn't mean I don't consider and reconsider and turn it inside out and upside down but the truth is I usually know in the first instant. When I left the *Sunday Business Post* to go to Granada TV's *World in Action* in Manchester, I was leaving a full-time job with a new and thriving paper for a six-week contract in another country, a television job for which I had no experience, in a city where I knew nobody. The decision was done and dusted in moments.

Indeed it was that decision that sparked this one. After the TV programme on the beef industry was transmitted in May 1991, I was offered a proper contract with *World in Action,* which again required only moments for me to accept. This was a different prospect altogether, not about telling one story but about building a career in television in the UK. The brand, *World in Action*, was too compelling to walk away from and I felt I could learn a lot.

That beef programme followed me for years. First there was the tribunal of enquiry at which I had to give evidence and face down the inquisitors who wanted me to reveal my sources. I refused – naturally – and refused again the next day, having been sent home to consider the matter. I finished my evidence and went back to work and gave birth to my first daughter five months later. Bear in mind that the programme had cooperated fully with the enquiry, furnishing written evidence, documentation and anything that was not confidential. We had quite a lot of relevant research but instead I was 'damned' for keeping the names of the sources to myself. That was November 1992 and the 'shoot the messenger' brigade had already reared their heads.

In August 1994, a warrant was issued for my arrest. The story was broken to me not by the relevant authorities but by Veronica Guerin, in a phone call from the *Sunday Independent*. I was completely taken aback and I think she was too. I still remember stumbling around the *World in Action* office that Friday afternoon – I'm sure it was a bank holiday weekend in the UK – explaining it to colleagues, who were equally stunned. The lawyers intervened when the story was official and an arrangement was made for me to return to Ireland 'to be arrested'. Now, that seems utterly ridiculous, but it really was the only way to deal with it – otherwise I couldn't return to Ireland safely.

The arrest was followed in January 1995 by the trial. We had lost our SC, Niall Fennelly, to the European Courts and he was replaced with the wonderful (late) Kevin Haugh and his junior Felix McEnroy whom I knew from schooldays. Michael Kealy was our solicitor, as he had been at the tribunal. We argued that evidence given at a tribunal could not be used as evidence in a court of law; the judge intervened from the bench and the case collapsed. We had won and I walked free from that hard bench.

It was fairly clear to me, from the support of the NUJ and BECTU (the UK Broadcasting, Entertainment, Cinematograph and Theatre Union) from the Gardaí, the court staff and even the jury that everybody thought this was a farcical exercise and that I was simply being made an example of. Public support was enormous. People wrote to me, stopped me in the street, stopped my husband and sent good wishes to the family. They recognised that I had been brave in the first instance to stand up and tell the story, to dare to put Charles Haughey's face on a meat hook and say that there were irregularities and that there was closeness between big business and politics. And they knew that I was willing, if not exactly keen, to go to jail if necessary, but that I would allow no witch hunt of those who had been brave enough to come forward to tell me their stories.

That sense of standing up, of doing the right thing, made an impact on me. More important was the fact that members of the public appreciated it, enough to stop and tell me so. They knew things were wrong and that those in power were abusing it and they knew that I had been scapegoated for daring to reveal this. How many others stood trial as a consequence of the revelations on that programme? I was the only one.

Campaign Diary

Tuesday 24 March

It's just three days to launch – at the party's annual conference in Mullingar. I have a long telephone conversation with D, who says what he always says – that sometimes things are meant to be. He is always calm and cuts to the chase He asks if it really feels right, inside? I know what he means. It's not about the risk, the strangeness, the chance – it's just about me and my gut instinct. He reminds me of what he has said before: that doors are closed in order for others to be opened. Well, several doors have closed recently. He says that we are 'lucky' sometimes to be asked to do these things; that in his experience there are often three opportunities and that's it. Well I'm on number one but somehow I don't feel like waiting till number three comes round. It's a long call – forty-five minutes – but after talking to him I do feel that it's the right thing to do.

There are some people you have to check in with before you make a big decision and there have been quite a few this time. I've pretty much checked in with all of them and some of them are probably fed up now as there has been vacillating on my part, especially as the deadline approaches. It hasn't helped, having to keep quiet about it – because the party would like to keep the announcement as a surprise for the party conference and that means saying nothing to many people, which in some strange way means the whole thing isn't real. And won't be until the actual moment – which allows my brain time to question everything again, time to change my mind, time to withdraw. But then I'm not the withdrawing kind.

Thursday 26 March

It's the day before the party conference and I feel sick and don't want to go but as I am saying this I am out getting my hair cut and panic shopping. I'm not very good at panic shopping, then I go home and have a panic wardrobe moment. Do I have enough clothes? Does any woman! I haven't the faintest idea what I need because in all the consultation about what this might mean for me and what will happen with the launch and how the campaign might be run, I forgot entirely to find out what events there are at conference and what kind of clothes I should have. Wisely, the only moment of wisdom in the entire day, I decide that it's far too late to worry now and that what I have will have to be sufficient. By dinner, I have a serious case of the wobbles and can't eat – quite literally. My husband's birthday is marked in a rather haphazard fashion but, as he has bravely signed up to the whole thing, he is kind about it. By now the secret is growing out of proportion. When I attempt to assess why I am anxious, I come back to the same place in my head; I am a journalist and have guarded my independence fiercely for more years than I care to remember. In just one day, I will give that up. So I guess it's a good reason to have the wobbles. And it's not simply a matter of giving that up, it's giving it up to go out there and be a candidate, to be a face on the lamp posts, to have my name on the ballot paper, to have something to say, to have the right thing to say, to do something useful, to offer an alternative, to be credible, to stand up and say enough is enough and I don't want this country to continue to be ruined and to stand by while it happens. No pressure then!

Friday 27 March
I finish the piece for the *Irish Daily Mail* on why I want to run. Pressing the send button calms me.

In 1995, after I stood trial in the Circuit Criminal Court for not revealing my sources to the Beef Tribunal, people came up to me on the street to thank me for taking a stand, for revealing truths and for not being afraid. Fourteen years later, people still thank me and still say they thought it was important that the truth came out.

These comments have always mattered to me because they confirm to me that Ireland is full of people who care about the truth, who care about honesty and integrity and who are comatose listening to and watching politics and public life being dominated by those who have forsaken the truth for a quick fix.

My personal 'small p' politics have been clear for a long time. I believe in equality and honesty and I have kept it at the core of programmes I have produced and articles I have written. My decision to enter politics was influenced by that core belief and by having shaken hands with people who want a fairer Ireland, who want new voices in the political system and who want to be able to trust those new faces with their vote.

Of course there is no political party that matches any one person completely – that's called 'Do it yourself your way'– but democratic parties, with their clashes, personalities and flaws remain the best system we have to thrash out a way to live our lives. As the Labour Party does not specialise in bronze, silver or gold circles and is committed to transparency, to politicians having to reveal their interests and to the control of political donations, it's no big surprise that I have chosen to run with the Labour rose as my symbol.

And why Europe? Well I've grown up with Europe and I love the idea of the shared culture and heritage of such a wonderful continent. I still remember the pride and excitement of our going 'decimal', when I had to count out 'new pennies' on the bus to school. We all embraced travel, work and education in Europe and appreciated for the first time that dinner could be something other than spuds, meat and two veg. The best cappuccino I ever had was on the side of the road in northern Italy in the middle of the night when the Magic Bus I was on displayed its lack of magic and broke down for two hours. Now I can go to any town in Ireland, from Ballina to Bruff, and expect a decent coffee.

Europe is now absolutely part of our lives; it's not the bogey-man in the corner with straight bananas and an end to neutrality. For me, to be a member of the European Parliament offers a real chance to try to bring the smell of Spanish oranges and the snow of the Alps to

Ireland, to make the connections that are there already matter. And, as the forum for the biggest challenges facing us, our economy and our environment, decisions made and laws passed in Europe will be crucial for all of us – for my children, for all our children.

Seeking to be a candidate is no easy choice. The idea of seeing my own face stuck on a lamp post is very peculiar. Seeking election means that more than your face will be torn from a lamp post: being ignored, ranted at or shouted at is all in a day's work. The personal rough and tumble is a given, even though I've yet to measure the thickness of my own neck. No, what makes it difficult is the enormous responsibility of offering to serve the public. Deciding to stand means I accept that and will aim to put my best foot, body and brain forward.

Yes, I am putting the camera down for now, but if I am elected to serve in the European Parliament that won't stop me continuing to ask difficult questions and challenging people: God knows I've had years of practice! Becoming an MEP would allow me to use my journalistic skills in a new way, standing in a different position in the room to carry on the challenge for truth and honesty.

I've seen the best and worst of the media and I'm pretty confident I will see the best and worst of politics if I am elected. But as a journalist at heart, I will always be striving for the truth. If I am elected and fail to bring some of that truth into the system, then I will have failed

– not just myself but those who voted for me believing that I will.

Irish Daily Mail, Saturday 28 March 2009

There. It's out there now. I've said it out loud even though it won't appear until tomorrow. I sort out my clothes and pack, then realised I am delaying and delaying: talking, drinking tea, sweeping the floor. Now I'm not calm any more. I feel ill and don't want to go now but I say goodbye and get in the car. Paul and I decided not to take the whole family – that we don't want them to be 'props' – but that they might come when I am launched in Sligo: I am aware that I do have to wait for fourteen days before I actually become the official candidate, in case someone else in the Labour Party comes forward.

I drive to Mullingar and it's all a bit of a rush now because I delayed. I am introduced to Mags Murphy, who has been designated my 'minder'. She is calm and welcoming and explains what will happen next. God help her – dealing with a woman in panic. The secret seems to have held, so we don't delay in the hotel lobby. Of course, in my confusion, I leave half my stuff in the car so I have to sneak back downstairs, across the lobby, then back into the hotel again, hoping no one will see me. I do an embargoed interview with Newstalk so they get the first public version, then we head for the press conference, or the unveiling, as it has been called. I have been amused by this expression since I first heard it as I thought it was only plaques and statues that get unveiled but no, it's about to happen to me! Fortunately no one has to whip a cloth off or press a button. Instead I am flanked by party leader Eamon Gilmore and party president Michael D Higgins. Eamon steps forward and makes the announcement and says how proud and pleased the party is that I am running and that the party now has four good candidates to contest the Euro elections. Then it's my turn. To be honest, I don't remember exactly what I say. I try to be coherent, to say that I believe in Europe and that I'm proud to be standing with the Labour Party. I can see Mags smiling at the back of the press group, trying to persuade me to smile. I obviously have my serious face on! There are plenty of questions but nothing hard or harsh, then one amuses me – 'When did I join the party?' How about five minutes before I stood here!

All this is followed by a round of handshakes and constant smiling. I've no idea who I'm shaking hands with as I am still in a daze but what I am aware of is how warm and welcoming people are and how many people say, 'Thank you,' to me for coming forward to run. It had never occurred to me that people would say that but I have never been a member of any political party and some of them have been candidates and know what is ahead of me!

Then it's upstairs to the makeshift studio and an interview with RTÉ Radio's *Drivetime*. Now that *is* surreal for me – it's Friday evening and usually I am in studio, doing the review of the week with other guests. Now I'm on the phone, being asked why and what and when. I know for sure that I have crossed that line – I'm on the other side. Mary Wilson asks me if I will vote yes to Lisbon and I say yes.

Paul, my husband, rings me afterwards and says he was in a newsagent's in Sligo and Kevin, the man behind the counter, says, 'That journalist Susan O'Keeffe is running for Europe for the Labour Party,' so Paul says, 'Yes, that's my wife.' So I guess we both had a surreal moment at the same time. I get through it all and finally, exhausted, I go to my room. Now I am hungry so order is restored and I spend some time replying to texts of good wishes, some from those who knew and some from those who are completely surprised. So far only one person says I am a 'mad fool' but it was said kindly – I think. Perhaps you do have to be 'a mad fool' in the first place.

Saturday 28 March

Up early; I need to meet people and generally 'be seen' so am brought to the front row of the conference hall. Ruairi Quinn is speaking and takes a moment to say the 'party is honoured' to have me. Again it feels surreal to be in a hall full of people and to be singled out. I am asked to sit on the platform and am welcomed again and this time Brendan Howlin nudges me to stand up and wave. If it's normal in political circles, it seems utterly abnormal to me but I manage to do it without falling over feet or seat. I am entirely uncertain about what I have done: a night's sleep has not clarified my thoughts.

I go to have my photo taken with first-time women candidates and Eamon. There are a lot of us, which is good given the extreme shortage of women in politics in Ireland. This is followed by a Labour Women's lunchtime meeting. Mags introduces me to all the groups, who are gracious and welcoming. There seems to be millions of them but that's because I don't know them and they know me. Sidestepping food, I go back to the RTÉ studio to take part in the Bowman programme. I am anxious, never having been interviewed by him before, but it goes fine, although somehow we end up talking about conspiracy theories.

Mags organises a brief strategy meeting with the election co-ordinator, David Leach, and the press adviser, Paul Daly, largely because I feel it will stop me panicking if I know what's going to happen next. I'm not used to not knowing or having to wait for other people to outline the next move and it's difficult to be so in the dark. I can imagine what a campaign is but, well, that's not quite the same as having to run one. The meeting is necessarily brief but it makes me realise just how short the time before the election is in real terms. Can you have a strategy at all in a constituency of this size with only weeks left and a candidate who doesn't even know all the people in the party, never mind know the party's policies on any number of things – Common Agricultural Policy, immigration, Palestine…I am a bit anxious about the lack of detail and think I will have to make it all up myself. They have things to say but no time to say them. One thing we are aware of is how Declan Ganley will influence our constituency but we agree that we will not let him monopolise and lead – in so far as we can. It will be interesting to see how that plays out.

I am glad to see my sister, Anne, who has arrived with moral support and some additional wardrobe items. This is timely because Mags announces that I have a photo shoot for posters and leaflets for the campaign. I haven't time to be surprised and we carry as many items as we can into the photographer's temporary studio. I'm grateful that there is proper make-up, courtesy of RTÉ, and we manage to turn the session into a laugh with endless smiling and conversations about smiling and how difficult it is to smile on cue. I blame the nuns for teaching us to be serious! The photographer is patient and understanding: I hope he's dealt with worse than me! There is a photo op with fresh red roses; Liz McManus pins a rose on my shirt and tells me to 'enjoy the campaign', which sounds like good advice. She adds that, 'Everyone should do it once,' – stand – so they understand the process.

I have some time in the hall again to hear the internal debate about reform of the party which, I realise much later, is very significant. The vote is carried easily but with some spirited speeches in opposition. I notice that, like the number of women involved, there seem to be a lot of younger members and candidates and that's great. In truth there should be far more, here as everywhere, but at least in the room the balance is not skewed completely towards the greys. Politics in Ireland has to find a way to appeal to people under thirty but as long as it still feels itself in the last-century frame of civil war, young people will turn their backs and rightly so! It's enough to make me feel reluctant about politics but my hope is that this frame is changing, that the influx of non-Irish will encourage that move, along with the changing economic circumstances which will perhaps encourage people to concentrate on what is happening now and what is needed now, rather than on who our fathers knew and voted for. Having one foot stuck in the past makes progress oh so slow and not very smooth.

That evening the queue forms for Eamon's speech, which will be televised. There is a very positive atmosphere. I find I don't have to queue; along with the other candidates I am invited to sit in a kind of square around Eamon's podium. I find myself sitting next to Martin Schulz, chair of PES group, another organisation that I am only beginning to understand. It's the Party of the

European Socialists and the biggest group in the European Parliament. Labour MEPs sit with the PES. Martin is impressive and we chat for a while, then there are speeches and awards to long-serving members of the party, which make me feel like an interloper. Deputy leader Joan Burton introduces all the European candidates and there is a big round of applause for me. Eamon's speech is strong and rousing and without unnecessary theatrics but it does feel odd sitting 'in' the speech rather than reporting on it. Are my critical faculties still intact? At the end there is cheering and I am raised on to the podium to be photographed next to Eamon. It's quite an achievement as I'm wearing heels and a skirt not designed for clambering. I'm beginning to learn that photos are important, especially photos with the party leader.

There are more photos with various people after that, then lots more handshaking and a chance for a glass of wine and a stool to lean on. I am more tired than I could imagine. It's all so new, as are the faces. It's like being in a foreign country where you don't speak the language. Then suddenly my cousin Pat turns up from Kilbeggan. How nice of him to come and what a surprise.

We fall into conversation at the bar and people recount stories about previous elections and previous party leaders and funny moments and arguments and people getting lost and who knew whom and alliances and enemies and it makes me realise that a political party is a large family: dysfunctional, with cousins, black sheep, heroes, hard workers, affairs and broken promises. I've just joined one and in an afternoon have been made to feel welcome, with no judgement passed about my lack of knowledge about this particular family. Several people tease me and ask if I intend to write a book! In that brief conversation, it seems to me that several books could be written as old and new swap memories and I try to work out who is jostling for position and who is happy to sit back. I know I am still looking in because I have only a handful of stories to tell. Michael D's wife, Sabina, says she is looking forward to me coming to Galway and promises to look after me. I talk at some length to Alex White, who is running in the Dublin South by-election and is working hard and feeling confident that the effort is beginning to pay off. I decide that enough is enough and head for bed, losing an hour to summer time as I go. I leave plenty of people behind: the party conference is as much a party as a conference.

Sunday 29 March

There is certainly an air of the morning after the night before although the conference hall is fairly busy. I meet Barry Desmond and Emmet Stagg at breakfast and am then introduced to councillors and candidates from Sligo. I haven't seen Barry Desmond since I interviewed him for the beef programme when he was an MEP. By now I have met all the European candidates who previously stood for Labour in the North-West: Ger Gibbons, Hugh Baxter and Ann Gallagher. The advice varies from keeping an eye on what we spend to making sure I never canvass alone, never stand alone anywhere and never abandon a conversation with a member of the public. The significance of this is lost on me as I eat toast and read the Sundays but I will remember the words later. People insist that I am brave and I nod and say yes but again the significance of that comment is lost on me.

Now it's time to pack up and leave and go back to the real world. I realise as I assemble all the bits that it's been a bubble of a weekend where everybody has been warm and lovely and I have been made to feel important – which is why parties have conferences, to meet and galvanise and motivate. On my way back from Mullingar I nip into a supermarket and realise how normal it is: people doing a bit of shopping and not in the slightest bit concerned about politics, candidates – or me. The last two days suddenly feel like a product of my imagination because there is no campaign and I am still not the candidate. Is it all some kind of practical joke? Or is it that it matters hugely to politicians and not at all to the public and that this disconnect means politicians never look or feel like they are singing from the same hymn sheet because they are all consumed by what they do and think and need, and forget that everyone else simply isn't.

I race to Sligo and am in time to see my youngest daughter Eva's ballet awards. What a pleasure to see so many happy little faces and proud parents. These are the moments to savour and it was worth the rush back from bubble land. Watching a political programme on RTÉ later that night I am suddenly struck by the realisation that people will always vote the way they have done: they don't care that there might be a better or different way unless that new message can be steam-rollered home with maximum publicity – as achieved by Barack Obama. Saturation is more likely to work – whoever you are – and that's what Declan Ganley will aim for because he can afford it. I decide to amuse myself and see how much tea I drink between now and the end of the campaign.

Monday 30 March

I do an interview with Ocean FM here in Sligo about why I am running and why I chose Labour. That's all pretty fine. A guy called John calls in and disses all journalists and says we are to blame for the state of the economy and the gloom and we have not helped and people themselves are to blame for being in debt. I realise straight away that lots of people will come out of woodwork to find something bad to say and that's always a good line – 'bloody journalists' – and who can blame them. I do an afternoon interview with Highland Radio who are confused and think the embargo for my launch is today!

Tea tally: 3

Tuesday 31 March

I do an interview with Midwest Radio. They ask about the gap of knowledge about Europe and how remote Europe is and how do we bridge that. This is a good question and hard to answer in a way that will make a difference. It's a problem that everyone talks about it and everyone recognises but we are no closer to solving. I certainly don't know what the solution is, except that someone needs to take responsibility for it. I go to my first branch meeting in Sligo; it's to ratify Veronica Cawley as a candidate. She is a councillor and the current mayor of Sligo. It's good to meet the local members and to see at first hand what 'grass roots' politics means: people at local level keeping this party and every other party going. Without them, great aspirations, promises and policies are worthless. There has to be a machine to mobilise the party and this is my first brush with it. My minder from the conference, Mags Murphy, is here as the party's candidate officer. She chairs the meeting and follows the formalities for the ratification. I make a short speech, there are a couple of other speeches and it's done. I then shake hands and talk to people and drink tea. I realise afterwards that that's what candidates have to learn to do: 'work the room', whatever the room is, shake hands, say a few words and move on. There is a certain art to it and I'm sure that practice makes perfect but since I genuinely enjoy meeting people and have spent a lifetime talking to and getting to know strangers, this is a part of the job I should enjoy. Remembering people's names is also part of the art and that's harder, because you can be introduced to ten in a row and never hear their name again in the entire time you are in the room. I also realise that as the Euro candidate I am expected to speak at all these meetings so I need to think hard about what I want to say. This is my opportunity to introduce myself to the party on the ground. Will they like me or want to canvass for me or even vote for me? Well, they certainly won't if I don't make an effort.

Tea tally: 5

Wednesday 1 April
No, it's true. I'm still running. I get my new email address for the party so at least I can contain all that stuff somewhere separate from my real life. I hear from my friend Julia who says I must be only candidate who caused the fall of a government before I got elected! Good line. I try to work on my radio documentary for RTÉ but am too distracted to concentrate. Mags and I have already had a 9am meeting in town where we choose the photos for the posters. That was quick! I think the photos make me look old and it's hard to ignore this. In fact I'm learning how much the

image stuff matters. If you're going to go out there, you have to do it by the book. Turning up in scruffy jeans won't wash. Voters want their public representatives to look respectable so it's the least we can do if we are trying to represent them. Unfortunately, I can't do much about my age although this hasn't stopped lots of advice. We do manage to laugh a bit about it and, to be fair, the photographer has done a very good job. It's just – who likes looking at themselves? We also talk about my non-existent team. I need a campaign manager and a couple of people whom I've asked aren't free and a couple of others the party asked aren't free either. This is making me fret because I am impatient and want to get on.

Our local council candidate for Dromore West, Alwyn Love, comes to visit in the evening. He tells me about his campaigning and how much canvassing he has been doing over the months. He really has been working hard and he offers to help me when I start canvassing, which is kind. It's his first time running too and, listening to him, I begin to understand some of the politics of politics and this is when I want to close my ears as I have enough to try to get my head around. I am starting to put some time aside to read about the Lisbon Treaty, the European Commission, how the European Parliament works and what the functions of an MEP are. I think it's important to understand the role even though it's always more difficult to talk about a job you've actually never done. I'm lucky enough – I've been to the EU, the Parliament and the UN, so I have strong images in my head about how these organisations work. And over the years as a journalist I have read various reports relating to Europe or the UN as research for programmes so it's not *all* new. Somehow it feels new because I have to relate it to myself first, then try to make it coherent to the public which, as we already know, is not hugely engaged with Europe.

Tea tally: 6

Thursday 2 April

Drive to Mullingar to meet Mags and local TD Willie Penrose and Billie, his sidekick, and very efficient 'representative on earth'. We eat dinner and we watch the stars come in to an enormous local fashion show at the hotel. It's weird to be back less than a week later at the same hotel I started in and to feel so different. Willy watches everyone and sitting with him is a completely different experience from just having a meal because he knows who everyone is and how they are connected and they all know him. We meet Biddy White-Lennon on the way out: it's that strange moment you meet someone very well known and you think you must know them until you remember you know them from television. When I worked at Granada TV, we used regularly bump into Coronation Street stars in the lift or the club. After my first star-struck response, I realised that they preferred to be treated normally so we would just chat with them and avoid all mention of 'the Street' or 'the Rovers' Return'. Willy then gives me the tip that if people say as you reach the gate on your way out, 'I'll look after you,' they never mean it. Equally I should watch out for the FFers who keep you talking endlessly so that you can't canvass or offer you tea to make you waste even more time. I get the feeling I haven't the faintest idea what's out there.

We all head off for Delvin to the ratification for Dan McCarthy, who's seventy-nine and wonderful. It's the formal procedure for

Dan to be the candidate in the local elections. It's a back room in a bar but there's huge enthusiasm – never mind the wallpaper which is new but circa 1957 in fashion terms. Everyone speaks very warmly of him and he feels like the real deal: he left school at thirteen and has worked in the community ever since. He's all scrubbed up in his suit and shiny shoes – methinks he would be more comfortable in wellies. When my turn comes I say that since I left Ireland, farmers have been forgotten and that in the rush for property we seem to have turned our backs on what was familiar to us. I tell them about my farming roots, which seem to play well but they would, wouldn't they? I say I could take lessons from Dan and in fact that is true. Then Willy speaks about the need for change and the damage done. He says I was wonderful and have been to prison! That James Connolly would be proud of me (which got a cheer) and that 'Europe needs Susan more than Susan needs Europe'. I think it will be hard to beat that line. Then we broke up and chatted and shook hands. There was one lovely old woman who has a carer but who knows for how much longer and she's worried. That's one of Willy's big things – carers – and he's threatened to chain himself to Leinster House if they touch the carer's allowance. I'm minded to join him.

Tea tally: 5

Friday 3 April
I talk to K, who says she might be interested in helping and that she will talk to her brother at the weekend and call me on Monday. Then Mags calls to say she will be my campaign manager. I'm not sure that's a good idea because she's very busy and I don't know how they can spare her or whether I will ever be able to get hold

of her when I need her. It all seems too slow to me and I would have thought someone would have come forward by now but no one has. When I see what Alan Kelly – already a Senator and Labour's Euro candidate in Munster – has, I feel a bit left out and behind but then he has been organised for a long time and has worked hard. I knew it would be last minute but this doesn't feel right to me and I'm often right about these things. Mark rings to make sure I'm OK. I express a small reservation but find it difficult over the phone and don't want to be ungrateful. This is uncertainty writ large and impatience on my part. I don't want to be the candidate without a campaign.

I drive to Crossmolina, to David Moffatt's first meeting in his father's pub. David is our new council candidate for the Ballina area. I see how drink plays a part in all these things, how meetings are often held in pubs, the focal point of communities in small towns. No wonder politics and drink go hand in hand. I don't think having a meeting in a church hall or sports hall would be quite so attractive. David admits he's not very clued up on Europe but he does have his heart set on winning the Ballina seat and he makes a good speech. Bernie Courtney is there too – she's running for Castlebar. I say it's a great night for Labour in Mayo – with three new faces – and a fresh start for the party in the county. However, I don't think too many people there will actually vote Labour. David used to be involved with FF so it's a bit of a strange switch, I think. But then that's politics. I get my tea tally up: I have tea before and tea afterwards! With breaded chicken and chips – a huge improvement on the old fashioned rubber chicken; this man spares no expense.

Tea tally: 7

Saturday 4 April and Sunday 5 April

Hurrah, respite, so I read some material. It's hard because there is so much to know and it is hard to know what is right to know. Difficult, a bit like sitting an exam – but in what subject? Farming, fish, the economy, tourism and I continue to be distracted by my own radio documentary about millers and the history of milling in Ireland which I should have finished but haven't, and it's getting harder to finish. I will have to be disciplined and set aside a day to finish it properly. I have really enjoyed meeting the people and threading through the history of mills so I owe it to them not to allow this campaign to distract me from their story.

Pressure is coming on me to draft what I want to put on my leaflet. I am so cynical about leaflets normally. They come through the letterbox and I give them a quick look, a quick read if they seem interesting, then I chuck them. From that point of view I suspect I am like everyone else and I think in my heart that I can't make mine so different that people will take a different view of it. This is what I come up with:

I stand

- for honesty not lies
- for constituents not cronies
- for work not words
- for courage not cowardice
- for strength not sleaze
- for you not me
- for a better Ireland for all of us

But when we talk about it we decide it doesn't quite work even if all the sentiments are valid. So I try again:

I stand for an Ireland

- built on community, not cronies
- built with good neighbours, not golden circles
- building jobs, not bailing out bankers
- building a green future, not a greed future
- building hope for a better Ireland

We decide that this will work but then I realise there are two sides to the leaflet so I have to fill the other side, which is harder. By now quite a number of my friends have been asking what do I stand for and it's difficult to answer in the European context because the answer seems to be about Ireland and what we want. I don't think it will work if I write a big proposition about Ireland's place in Europe.

On the other side:

Susan O'Keeffe is an outstanding campaigning journalist whose pursuit of the truth exposed corruption in corporate Ireland. She lives in Sligo with her husband and three children and is standing for Europe in Ireland North-West on behalf of the Labour Party.

Tea tally: 6

Monday 6 April

I receive a copy of Eamon Gilmore's fundraising letter; it reminds me I need to write one, a personal one to people I know, and how important funds are. Without money, there will be no campaign. However I have to wait to be ratified. That's my shelter for now. I really am dreading asking for money.

I get a nice phone call from Buncrana from Margaret, the woman who owned the B&B where I stayed during the making of the RTÉ documentary on Frank Shortt, to say well done and to wish me well. That was really nice. Alwyn Love rings to say I could have a poster at the church next Sunday but I'm not sure because I'm not the candidate yet. Can I get a clarification? Eh. No. Can I get a jpeg of my photo to make a poster? I have asked a hundred times; think I'm asking in the wrong place. Ring Mags: no answer. She has promised a draft diary today but none so far; hardly surprising, there is a million other bits of paper to put in place as well as liaising with other candidates, just to get me up and running. K texted to see if am OK so have arranged to call her tomorrow as my instinct is still that not enough is happening, although this may be partly because am feeling guilty myself about doing so little. I got a very useful mail from D, with some good headlines on farming to have at my fingertips, also a message from old friend Katy saying wow and surprised but not really!

It's the eve of the budget and there is huge tension. Already Fianna Fáil has made a bags of it: axing five of the twenty junior ministers but saying they all have to reapply for their jobs. How long will that take, what a mess and how much time and money will that cost? Can they do nothing right? Then Dermot Mannion resigns from Aer Lingus. I wonder what secrets he could reveal!

Eamon Gilmore is sticking to his line that the budget must be fair and that it must create jobs and hold on to the ones there are. It strikes me that this is a brave approach and that jobs are what it's about. Every time you see Eamon Gilmore he says jobs, job, jobs. It's a mantra but will it pay off? Should there be more detail in the mantra? Has it been road-tested with audiences? Will it stick? There is much discussion about a possible general election but is that really possible? Is there enough anger among wobbly FFers – that's what's needed. Or will we all be chaining ourselves to Leinster House? Mags sends me the draft diary and it's good to see a basic structure.

Tea tally: 3

Budget Day, Tuesday 7 April

I sit and listen to the whole thing. It's having to watch your own country tearing itself apart that's hard, tearing up its own book of plans, knowing that it's you – and more importantly, your children – who will suffer as a consequence of this day and all the days that went before this one. I am thinking that if I were sick or old or had a child with difficulties of any kind how angry I would be. Richard Bruton's speech seems to me to be a bit disorganised but heartfelt; Joan is on form and gets better as she warms up. I have to go and write a piece for the *Mail*. I wander round for a bit, not quite sure how to approach it because there is so much to say. In the end I opt for the non-apology of the government and their 'with hindsight' arrogance. Watching Bertie Ahern was almost the most interesting part: there he was on the backbenches with his hand resting on his chin, looking glum, pensive, miserable. Actually, I don't care how he feels. He ought to be ashamed of himself and I'm not sure he is. The biggest question posed by this budget is the banking one and the creation of a bad bank. I feel that it's already a lie, that book value debts will turn out to be higher, that the banks will need more capital at some point and that nationalisation might have been safer.

Yesterday the government failed to apologise for its part in our downfall. Finance Minister Brian Lenihan talked instead about the wisdom of hindsight, and how we know now that the housing boom should have been curtailed.

But we knew then, Brian. Lots of people were talking about it – economists, pundits, politicians, punters. Actually, Brian, the dogs on the street were talking about it but then, people like you are not on the street very often so maybe that's your excuse. Hindsight? Don't make me weep. Your collective government eye was nowhere to be seen, least of all policing or controlling a property boom which made you look good and kept you in power.

Instead while you were listening to your friends in the Galway tent, Ireland 's future was starting its slow trickle down the drain. Yesterday in Leinster House, the trickle turned to a torrent as all of us watched our futures flushed away by a budget which will tax us whichever way we turn. Today our incomes are falling and in the longer term we can see more of the same as your accountants and actuaries promise more chopping and shredding at Christmas; especially if you're on social welfare and even if you're a saver.

We all know the figures don't add up and that we need to pay up but, foolishly, we thought we might be paying up in a more creative way; real incentives for entrepreneurs, genuine initiatives for the unemployed, joined-up thinking between government departments, perhaps a shred of joined-up thinking between FÁS and the voluntary sector to encourage people to get involved at community level? What we needed with the gloom was some optimism, some sense of purpose, some galvanising of the nation – not just to empty its pockets but to pick itself up and get going again.

Silly us. We should have known better. After all, there was little creativity on show when times were good, so it was unlikely now, and the paucity of leadership since the Taoiseach took the job makes it impossible. Oh yes, you made a show of putting your own house in order first with your bit of tinkering with politicians' expenses and long-service pay. The dogs on the street know those cuts could have gone deeper. They know too that your promise of 'cleansing' the banks in future will not take one euro from those bankers who have pulled the whole financial system apart. Where was the knife for them?

Apologise? We don't want it now. It's far far too late for that. And your 'slash and burn' budget won't work, Brian, because the hole is getting bigger and you're still not listening.

Irish Daily Mail, 8 April 2009

Wednesday 8 April

I drive to Carrick-on-Shannon to meet Mags and Kevin Cunningham, who is to be director of elections. It's the first official team meeting and Kevin provides an agenda, which is useful. We agree that he is the boss so that's a lot easier for me and he strikes me as a guy who takes it seriously. He's done lots of number crunching, had a couple of focus group meetings and has thought about it a lot already and is determined to do the best he can. So we talk about possible meetings and diary appointments and wheres and whens and I'm glad I'm not trying to sort it out. It's a long meeting but it feels like progress, the doing of it rather than the thinking about it, as well as the cold realisation that politics is not just about having the right policy or being in touch with the public but about having bodies keen enough to do things, smart enough to know what they are and available to keep doing it. Local candidate John Feely joins us too, which is great because he is very enthusiastic and an old hand and it makes me feel less green when people are there throwing their lot in behind me: less green but more responsible.

I drive to Dublin and change my clothes in the hotel before the Pat Rabbitte vs. Declan Ganley debate about the Lisbon Treaty. It's the UCG alumni meeting and it's very well attended and very civilised. I don't speak – by choice. I want to see Ganley in action before I share a studio or platform with him; I also want to see what the debate on Lisbon throws up. Ganley's main argument before this audience is the 'deficit of democracy', which has the ring of truth but is not a strong enough pillar to build a movement on, never mind a party. Both speak well. Pat seems a bit tired and he tells me later that he had a late budget night as they crunched the numbers. He is good at staying calm and smiling, not obviously trying to score points. But he does score a few, trying to raise a few laughs here and there, which Ganley doesn't. Ganley also has quite a few plants in the audience, all of them very obvious and none very impressive. Ganley does concede to a journalist that he will stand down from the Lisbon 'No' campaign if he is not elected, which means he must be pretty confident. No pressure then…

I came away thinking I need to read the Lisbon Treaty again and again, that Ganley does know it like the back of his hand but that for all his knowing, his argument is quite weak. It certainly didn't captivate me, from an intellectual point of view. I wasn't sitting there thinking that his argument was valid and hard to dismantle, rather that he is quite good at talking. He certainly has physical presence, which he knows how to use. I suspect it was a fairly sceptical audience but I enjoy the fact that the debate stayed civilised and there was no screaming match, which would have served no purpose. I wonder how often the Lisbon Treaty will come up in the campaign. Will people think Europe, think Lisbon straight away?

Tea tally: 9

Thursday 9 April

There is a meeting in Labour Party HQ at 10am this morning. I already had breakfast at 7am with my 'off-radar' adviser to talk through Declan Ganley and canvassing and the importance of message. It's useful to say things out loud to someone who is non-party but knows about trying to persuade people to listen at least. We have a conversation about the value of negative campaigning –

to be against something – and the research suggests that it works, although I don't like the idea of it at all. No, that's not entirely true: I don't like the idea of personal campaigning and that won't really happen here. It is easier to be positive, except when you look at the government. I am also reminded that when people say they are apolitical, they are actually FG; I hadn't ever thought about that. She advises me to ask people for their name when talking to them so that the conversation can be more personal. That's not something we always do in conversation; in fact using people's names is something I associate with over-zealous social workers or counsellors. It always smacks of insincerity to me. One neighbour springs to mind: she simply put 'Susan' into every second sentence. But I suspect that this is good advice which needs to be applied properly.

The party meeting is useful. We discuss the logistics of postering: the putting up and taking down of them and where and who. It's a big job – especially the taking down. As a voter, I have just noticed posters, then ignored them altogether. I never stopped for a single second to think about the enormous logistical effort required to put them up, never mind where they should be positioned and how much it will cost. Then there are the leaflets, which are a big headache – my own and the ones of me with the councillors in this region. And there's the *litir um thoghchán*. The leaflet discussion is about the four seconds between the piece being picked up from the floor and its going into the bin and what, if anything, might be absorbed by a potential voter in that time. A four-second window: that's the reality of politics today.

I sign a load of nomination papers and try not to ask too many questions, remembering that I don't have to organise; it's about turning up. How efficient will it all be? How could I know? All I can see is that people seem to be putting in a huge effort and want it to work. There are endless diaries to be merged: Eamon Gilmore's with everyone's, mine with councillors, mine with other European candidates…it will become the movable feast of diaries as the time progresses. Somebody mentions a Labour Women's dinner for fundraising. That would be fun! Maybe in Dublin where Nessa Childers and I could divide the spoils between us! Nessa is Labour's candidate in Leinster and stands a good chance. And more importantly I now have a diary which is starting to fill at an alarming prospect as the reality of eleven spread-out counties begins to take hold. There are things I will have to do as opposed to things I might like to do and I know too that the local radio stations have yet to provide dates for debates. These will always take priority because they are the best way for candidates to talk to voters in such a large constituency.

I have a press meeting with Paul about ideas to build my profile a bit, nationally and locally. It's much more difficult because I know a lot of the journalists personally and I don't want to be asking them or appearing to ask for favours: that seems naff. We make a list and agree that I won't be asking anything – the calls will be made by someone else and we will wait to see what that might yield. There is no doubt that press is important because the constituency is so huge. I write my *litir um thoghchán* – it's pretty similar to other stuff because, again, who reads them? Yes, lots of people do, mostly those who are committed to politics or are genuinely interested in switching their vote. But the rest don't and it's hard to capture that market. You can't do silly things to grab their attention because then you get lambasted for being silly. I don't think I've quite cracked this yet: how to bring imagination to bear to win over potential voters without making a fool of yourself or insulting the voters' intelligence. It's no wonder a kind of sameness descends on all political leaflets: who wants to 'dare to be different'? Dare only if you know it will work and then, well, it's not a dare, is it?

I go on to meet a friend who has promised to help out, which is great. She is going to try and organise a music event and possibly a golf classic, which seems a bit odd. There is a large audience there that is disaffected at the moment, especially after the budget, and who would recognise me and possibly even like me and they probably play golf – it's a big sport in this part of the world. We shall see if that comes to pass but it's the second time golf has been mentioned so who knows!

Then on the MAC make-up counter in Brown Thomas for some new make-up. There's a queue of people who know me giggling at the idea of me and make-up but you have to do it. If I'm going to have to wear it, I'd better do it right. A very nice young man gives me a makeover which I can never hope to equal but it works. I spend some money, run away because BT is always tempting, then back to the Labour Party office to pick up the stuff I forgot – umbrellas, T-shirts, pens, key rings.

I ring Joe Queenan, managing director of Foxford Mills in Mayo, whom I met making the mills radio documentary. Many people in Ireland remember Foxford blankets, either the white with the blue stripe or the pink with the satin edge. I really enjoyed recording there as people had great stories about their blankets. The modern Foxford blankets are really stunning and are a sharp reminder of 'modern Ireland', with Foxford now cast as a 'lifestyle' brand rather than as a utilitarian item. We chat and I ask Joe if he is happy for me to visit on the campaign. He says yes, which is great, because I think he and his team represent what is needed to succeed in good times and in bad. They are so determined to keep the business going and they have raw enthusiasm, which I admire. I look forward to going back there. It's late now and the weekend traffic has already started so it takes me quite a long time to get home.

Tea tally: 5

Good Friday, 10 April
Today is the march to save cancer services in Sligo General. That's odd – to be behind the banners, not filming. It's years since I marched for anything. I've always been careful not to march because I think you can't really take sides if you're a journalist. True impartiality is difficult but at least that way you're making no public representations. I think it's potty that sick people will have to travel to Galway, especially as they will shut services in Sligo without putting sufficient additional facilities in place in Galway. It's a complete desertion of common sense. I spot some journalists I know and they spot me and can't help laughing. I can't blame them: it does seem strange. The speeches are defiant and angry and close with the warning that no services will mean no votes. That's probably true for most of those people there, maybe about a thousand. All the politicians are careful to turn up, although I don't think there are any other MEPs or Euro-candidates there. Labour is closely identified with this campaign even though it is non-party. Veronica Cawley makes a speech but as Mayor of Sligo, not as a Labour councillor.

People feel the hospital slipping away, especially after the Ennis Hospital report from yesterday which will pretty much shut that place down and seems to be driven by an agenda about closing small hospitals. There is no love lost for Mary Harney in Sligo, that's for sure. It rains by the end but that doesn't dampen spirits and means I get to heave the large red-and-white Labour Party umbrella in the air. Good advertising.

Tea tally: 7

Saturday 11 April

I turn down a church-gate collection opportunity in Strandhill. It's difficult because I am still not the official candidate, although I don't think anything will happen now to stop that from happening. I feel this is my last weekend off for quite a while. A friend has come to visit from Manchester and, selfishly, I would like to put politics to one side for a couple of days.

Tea tally: 4

Easter Sunday, 12 April

I don't really put politics aside because I've already committed to Alwyn Love. There is an early start with Alwyn to get to the church gates for the Labour Party annual collection. It's *his* collection but an opportunity for me to be seen in public. We go armed with a poster each but because it's the church the words 'Vote Number One' can't appear anywhere, which is entirely reasonable. Alwyn has kindly had a poster done for me as my official ones aren't ready yet. I think it's quite good, if unnerving, to have to look at your own face!

We start in Ballisodare at 9am and, along with long-time Labour member, John McCarrick, move around Alwyn's area till nearly 1 pm. It's quiet enough: people are going into church, mostly in a hurry. Some people give because they don't want to be rude. Some – mainly women – apologise for not having money with them. Some probably don't have it these days and some don't want to give to us. One man had his hand in his pocket, then realised who we were and said, 'I don't give to them.' But my neighbour came and gave me a hug and said thank you and wished me well and that was a good moment. Another man rolled down his window and said he lived in Dublin and was in the Labour Party and wanted to wish me luck and say thanks for standing. We didn't get any abuse, nor did I get warm wishes – they were reserved for Alwyn because people know him. It seems odd to collect without dialogue.

The thing that I hadn't anticipated was local FG and FF councillors and members donating, until I realise that all the parties donate to one another in the 'we're all in this together' spirit. I suppose that's a bit of 'gentlemen's rules'. At one church the priest told us off for being too close to the gates, so we had to move. At another, we collected as people came out and three men came and stood directly in front of me, effectively blocking my position off. Could I move? No, obviously. I just had to stand and smile. Two of the three gave me a few euro at the end. I don't know how much the morning raised but it's not in the Ganley league. The Labour Party has never had that base: the party tries to belong to the people and say that every euro counts, but in lean times even the euro are hard to come by. I don't think this election will see a big spend by any party, certainly not by Labour. The hard part is that you have ask them all again the next time.

The drive is interesting as I begin to grasp a bit about how the councillors operate and how large the areas are, how remote some of the houses are, what sort of local issues are raised and what kind of tricks can be played. It's only one perspective but good to hear as the grass roots are where support is built or lost.

I don't do any more today, just a bit of gardening, chatting to the neighbours. The sun shines but it's cool enough. It feels as if by the end of this week, another few hurdles will have been overcome and the real campaign will have started. Not much time for gardening then. Today was about a bigger hurdle – asking people for money, which I hate, and asking them for money for politics. I suppose people understand that parties have to be funded and fundraising is such an intrinsic part of our society, especially in rural Ireland, that I suspect the people being asked have less of a problem about giving than I have about asking. At least I've done it. Remember Hillary Clinton – a third of her time devoted to fundraising. Yes, I know she lost, but the point is that it's a vital part of campaigning. It's not simply about having something to say or believing in something or wanting to change things. It's about filthy lucre, as ever, but it feels more blatant somehow.

Tea tally: 8

Monday 13 April
And there I was thinking it was a day off but Veronica texts and asks if we could meet Kevin this evening. I see that they are willing to give of their time for me and that's great, so I say yes. We talk diaries and canvassing.

Tea tally: 7

Tuesday 14 April

I am officially the candidate. What a relief. Not that there seemed to be any real prospect of anyone else coming forward but it is important to follow party rules, especially when you seem to have appeared from nowhere.

Tea tally: 4

Thursday 16 April

I write to Minister John Curran to complain about the suspension of the scheme of community support for older people, which was done last week. It seems a paltry cutback to suspend these kind of benefits which make a difference to older people and indeed help to keep older people independent. The promise to protect the vulnerable from cutbacks is not being kept and the government goes for cuts that are 'under the radar', where those affected find it hard to mobilise.

Tea tally: 5

Saturday 18 April

Mullingar, bright and early. What a glorious day. Canvassing is easier when the sun shines. People are less grumpy: outside, in their gardens, on the street, not faces to the wind. We have tea and scones, yes, in the Park Hotel again! We set off and do two shopping centres. It's productive because people are strolling through and most don't mind being stopped to shake a hand. I pinch myself now. This is me, surrounded by Labour Party people, asking complete strangers to vote for me. All I can say is I wouldn't want to be FF at the moment. People are very cross, bewildered and upset. The woman in the vegetable shop says business is down but it depends on the price of potatoes: that's what sets the tone of business for her! And at the moment, well, prices aren't the best. In the shopping centre, business owners say people have gone up north. They're really angry about the VAT and how they're being cut off at the knees and they don't understand why the VAT decision can't be reversed. In truth, neither can I. If at the stroke of a pen, it can be raised, then it can be reduced too. The cross-border drain cannot be ignored: people will vote with their wheels and go for 'the day out' and fill the car and think nothing of it, then wonder why their own local shopping malls are turning to ghost towns. The government seems to have set its face against this reduction, despite the common sense aspect of it and despite the depth of the lobby in favour of change.

We walk down the main street and shake hands. A Fine Gael councillor tells us she will vote for me!

Someone shovels a bowl of soup into me at lunch and off we go again, this time out to the country with TD Willy Penrose and his brother Johnny, who is a local councillor. It's a great experience being out with them: They are so impressive. No lists, no props, no *aide mémoires*. I remember filming with Glenda Jackson once, during a general election, when she was standing for Labour in the London constituency of Hampstead and Highgate. She had quite a large entourage and a big list of names that she would consult walking in each gate and with fingers crossed that the list was still correct. In a city of more than ten million, there is no other way of canvassing, but it makes each knock a journey into the darkness. Here the Penroses know everyone on the road, their parents, family, cousins…I begin to understand how all politics is local, how knowing people intimately makes them feel important and cared for and how in Ireland there really is only one degree of separation. They don't bother with the houses where the vote is staunch for FG or FF. Time is of the essence and they are a well-oiled operation.

Happily for me, a few people know who I am because with the Penroses, it's easy to feel like a stranger. It's their turf and they've worked it hard over the years and built a machine that knows exactly what it's doing. But Willy says he remembers when there were only a few Labour Party supporters on this road. A couple of people are saying they will switch from FF. Never having canvassed I have no idea if this is normal for the opposition party. Besides, it's not a general election. Even if people are polite and engage in chat, do they shut the door and carry on and vote for someone else on the day? It doesn't feel like that but I have nothing to judge it against and it's best to guard against wishful thinking. I enjoy being out in the sun, meeting people, and it does feel like the campaign is starting, even if slowly and carefully.

Then back into town and hand over to councillor Mick Dollard. He takes me to the Dalton estate and, my God, does he own it. We whisk round it at a rate, shaking hands and smiling. Everywhere people are grateful to Mick for sorting out problems of all kinds. I think he's more than a councillor: he's a counsellor too. I have a nice cup of tea in one house. Here the main problems are housing and unemployment. Mick says he doesn't think the other councillors come into this estate very much and I imagine there isn't much left for them. People promise to vote: if I'm with Mick, they'll vote for me! It seems weird to be asking people to vote when you know their frame of reference doesn't really include Europe. It's a challenge to know how we might communicate that message in such a way that everyone gets it. No one seems to have pulled that off in twenty years so I don't imagine it's easy. Perhaps some people think it's not worth it. I do, but I don't know the answer and I may never know it.

I find myself at one point saying to Mick: 'You in the Labour Party.' Oh dear, I haven't quite got this party idea yet. It's quite a difficult thing to do – to switch from being me, myself, to being *us*, part of an organisation – when I've spent years *not* being part of an organisation – apart from the BBC, which was a different kind of thing. Billy picks us up and I have welcome tea and sandwiches in Billy's house and he drops me to the station. Mags has already gone to Dublin. The train is very late and I'm tired but it was a positive day and a good place to start.

Tea tally: 10

Sunday 19 April

Sunday is a day off from the campaign but, sadly, other work calls. It will be easier when I don't have other stuff in my head. B and A call and congratulate me. I point out that I've done nothing yet but people feel I *have* done something by saying I'll stand. I'm beginning to work out what the unreality thing is: it's the fact that I've never *done* the job so I don't really know what it is. I could have a good guess at it and I'd come close but I don't actually *know*. That's the fate of the first-time candidate, rather like the longest job application in the world for your first job.

The sun shines so that's a help…

Tea tally: 3

Monday 20 April

I work in the morning and Mags arrives at lunchtime. I'm not having a good day so it's hard for her to motivate me but that doesn't stop her trying. It's damp and cloudy and that's not helping. I feel separated from the campaign and I'm sure that's because I'm not the producer. Will I ever stop being the producer? I doubt it. Anyway we have a bit of fun trying on dresses. That's a laugh for me: when do I ever wear a dress? Sooner than I think! Time to get ready and get into town but first a quick voice-over for the radio documentary which is dragging itself to the end line. I have lots of really good material but I think it's the juxtaposing of something historical with the absolutely current that's confusing my brain. I don't think a programme has been made about mills before so I want to make sure I do the best job I can but there is a lesson here: finish one thing before you start another! The research is fascinating. Mills were the first factories in Ireland and the start of our industrial economy. In fact there were close to 5000 mills in the country by the beginning of the 20th century, for mustard grinding, flax, corn, wheat, gunpowder – a huge variety of different activities. All this activity with the simple power of water! Perhaps in twenty years' time we will be turning back towards that production model.

I arrive into the Sligo Southern Hotel: Eamon is there and the 'caravan': the photos, the candidates and the handshakes. It's the SIPTU nursing conference and Eamon is making the keynote address. He is good – enough anger, enough desire to change, enough sincerity. People like him. We chat afterwards. He reassures me about being bewildered and he mentions 'canditatitis'. I ask him to explain. He says I will know what it is on 6 June but I think I already know. It is a state of paranoia on the part of the candidate, induced by elections. Everyone talks about it, everyone warns about it and I see how hard it might be to avoid it. I don't want to be the centre of the universe but as the candidate I am willing to be the centre of the campaign.

I tell Eamon about working at *World in Action* and particularly about the programme about child abuse and the Catholic Church which, given the current climate, seems so long ago. The programme was *Sins of the Fathers*, which was broadcast in the summer of 1992. In many ways, it is the programme of which I am most proud, because it was so profoundly important and because it made a genuine difference to real people and to their lives. That's never easy to achieve but I felt that programme took a real stand against an organisation that was powerful and wealthy and in this instance, wrong. People have been critical of the fact that the programme was made in the UK. How shortsighted! The programme highlighted the fact that Catholic priests and brothers were abusing children and being protected from the law by the Church. It doesn't matter where it was made: our stories spanned Europe and the US and included Ireland, where trying to get cooperation for this story was a blood from a turnip moment.

Then, horror of horrors, I watch the RTÉ news at 9pm and there I am standing next to Eamon as he is interviewed. I can only say that I look like a witch – far too serious and far too haggard and, worst of all, nodding my head. Yes, the light was harsh, and it's hard to know how to stand when you're not speaking but, my God, surely I can do better than that. It's hard to smile when someone is talking about the serious state of the country is in – but my goodness, I didn't have to be *that* serious! It's probably the biggest lesson I've learnt so far. I should have been made to see myself sooner and I do need someone to tell me these things. I now have to learn how to 'stand by'. Whoever would have thought there was a skill to standing!

Mags, Paul and I, along with other party members, join Eamon at the Sligo Park Hotel and have a strategy meeting about the next day: about the radio interview with Ocean FM and what might come up and cancer services and our stance generally on hospitals and centres of excellence. Paul advises me to make sure that I get a share of the conversation because inevitably Ocean will concentrate on Eamon. Leaders aren't in town very often and the poll yesterday was favourable to him so he's of more interest than me! Good advice, hard to take, as this will be the first time I'm on air with the party leader and it would seem rude to interrupt him.

Tea tally: 4

Tuesday 21 April

Am really surprised to hear an item on *Morning Ireland* about Sean Ó Neachtain pulling out of the European race. The report mentioned Declan Ganley and Pádraig Ó Lochlainn of Sinn Féin and how they might benefit. So what happened to Fine Gael, Labour and Marian Harkin? By the end of the show, they name-check us but it seems an odd piece of reporting. It's an interesting change in the race and how will FF respond? Put in someone? Leave it to Paschal Mooney. There are rumours about why Ó Neachtain might have pulled out, rumours that Máire Geoghegan-Quinn might run, or even Éamon Ó Cuív. But nominating the latter would risk a by-election and Fianna Fáil are on thin-enough ice as it is. The truth is that it leaves them in a strange position.

I go to Ocean FM and meet Eamon. I've been told that the cleaner was brought in because Eamon was visiting! It is very clean and tidy, tidier than when I've been there in the past. We sit and indeed Eamon *is* the star performer but that's absolutely right in my book. I have my first real political moment when I start by saying our thoughts are with Sean Ó Neachtain today and how difficult it must be to have to pull out of a race! It's the courtesy of politics which is right and professional but still seems strange. A sticky moment comes when I'm asked first about the Labour position on Sligo General and the cancer services and a quick flash in my head wonders if this is a trip point for me. I say we support centres of excellence but that a line of death has been drawn across the country and that Sligo must not be excluded from the system as it will be if this goes ahead. The presenter, Niall Delaney, turns to Eamon and says, 'Is that Labour Party policy – a ninth centre of excellence?' Fortunately Eamon says, 'Absolutely, yes,' and I see how those moments can go horribly wrong. The value of last night's briefing comes home. Of course I would be used to preparing for interviews, just on the other side of the table. In that situation, it's fair to test the candidate and see if she's up to speed! Niall Delaney anchors a two-hour show on Ocean every week day between 9am and 11am and he has a real knack of getting under the skin of something. His questions are flinty rather than aggressive and he persists if he thinks he's being spun a spin.

Eamon and I are on air for about twenty minutes, which seems like a decent chunk of time. We drive into town to the parlour of Mayor Veronica Cawley, where she makes us very welcome.

My family is late (!) so a hasty decision is made to switch the order of business and start with the Save the Cancer Services delegation. I don't take part in the conversation but am glad to be there and listen to their concerns. They are very passionate and have campaigned hard to keep the breast-cancer services in Sligo. Their argument is simple: the surgeon and the system work well so why dismantle the service and make people travel around the country at their illest and most vulnerable. It seems like a bit of a no-brainer to me.

Then we have the official launch of my campaign and of me as the candidate. Eamon praises me as a person of 'the highest integrity and remarkable courage'. I find it odd still to hear people praising me for doing my job but realise that in politics, integrity matters a lot. Eamon also uses the occasion to call for Eircom to be taken back into public ownership as its privatisation 'has been a disaster'. I feel a bit under pressure when my turn comes but I do remember to thank my family and point out that they are running in this election too, something that is entirely true. I concentrate on community: what we have, our strengths, how that's what the future has to be about: building on community, not on moaning and complaining.

Then we go to the hospital to visit the oncology services. The staff explain what it will be like to make the transition effectively to two centres, Dublin and Galway, because some Sligo people will go to Dublin. Even the most basic things like the transfer of files will pose a challenge. They were manful in their explanation but I got the sense from them of quiet bewilderment: that the task ahead was truly daunting. They were being positive but not enthusiastic, putting on a bit of a brave face, I think. I don't envy their job, especially as the people they care for are really ill, at their most vulnerable and wanting only to be treated fairly. It's fine if you can afford to buy something better but many people can't and if we call ourselves a civilised society, we must care equally for those whose pockets are not deep. We met some people with cancer, who were sitting getting chemo. That's always hard. One was a farmer from Coolaney, who was smiling and praising the staff. It feels strange to be making a visit with this hat on, not asking a million questions, not trying to get to the bottom of it – just listening to people, trying to understand how they feel and absorbing the way it is.

We leave on schedule and drive to Carrick-on-Shannon. I'm struck by how tightly Eamon's team sticks to the schedule: I moan the whole way that I want a cup of tea but we can't stop because of the schedule. Now that I'm on Twitter, we Twitter that. Mags rings ahead and organises tea for when I get there, so that's a minor victory. We do the photos then – with and without swans – on the Shannon. I make a note to myself that skirts have their down side as Eamon and local council candidate John Feely have to 'assist' me to stand up again after I stoop down to feed the swans for the photo!

Then it's walkabout in the town and I shake hands and smile. I'm struck by the number of tourists in Carrick. It is such a pretty town but under normal circumstances you have no idea who is local or not. Shaking hands is a great way to get in under the skin of a place – town, factory or hospital. You find out quite a lot pretty quickly. One woman makes Eamon and me roar laughing by saying to him that he looks like the leader of the Labour Party. And we think we are communicators! Those who do shake hands have nice things to say, which almost doesn't help because that warm feeling is a bit of a danger: it may lull me into thinking nice comments translate into votes, which, given how far outside I am, is hardly likely. A smile is not a number on the ballot paper. People by and large are not rude – even to politicians – and this surprises me but I *am* with the party leader. His popularity is running high and that does translate on the street. People say to him, 'You're great on the telly, the way you talk.' The public does notice the difference between straight talking and straight lying and between honesty and spin.

It does make the whole process of campaigning more pleasant when people are not rude and antagonistic. I'm sure there were times in the past when the Labour Party would have had a less warm welcome. We visit the Bush Hotel, which is the first eco-friendly hotel in Ireland or England and I'm impressed that they are doing that. Some school kids ambush a photo on the street. It's a dare, I imagine, but it's all good-spirited. Eamon is quick to chat to them and put them at their ease. Other politicians might take offence but he takes it in his stride and makes a friendly moment out of it.

At 2pm Eamon's gone and we head for Westport. It's a glorious day and the countryside is beautiful. A good day to canvass. Out of the car and straight on to the streets with a new set of councillors. A new set of names and more pressing the flesh. The candidate, David Fallon, is a first-timer like me so I guess neither of us has the confidence really to push it.

I'm very struck by a man we meet on the Octagon in Westport. He tends to the flowers on the streets and he's a part-time fireman. He shows us his pay slip for the last quarter and points to the pension levy he paid: €300, I think. It's not the amount as much as the fact that he doesn't have a pension from that job!! He's completely cross. He says he's happy to pay his bit, that he knows he has to, but not like this. Especially on a day when junior ministers who lose their jobs will get severance of €53,000 each, for doing nothing, it seems a bit rich. I begin to wonder if the rats in the ship are grabbing every crumb and piece of caviar before they have to flee: that they know the game is up. We walk round town and see that people are angry. They don't say a huge amount, just that shake of a head, the 'can't believe it's so bad' gesture. Some people recognise me, a couple say they were FF but not any more and in the main we get a warm welcome. I love the shop full of fishing tackle and the woman with the white hair with the old-fashioned fruit, vegetables and drinks shop who's down to earth and friendly. I get to shake Marcella's hand: she of the chocolate shop we tried to visit the last time we were here. She's happy for me to talk her up as an example of someone out there doing something, following a dream and working hard. Marcella's Chocolate Haven is a good name too! We go into Matt Molloy's pub and are very tempted to stay!

When we get to the hotel Mags gives me a lovely necklace to mark the occasion, the day of my launch, and I am touched. I also feel energised by the fact that she is now fully on board and prepared to juggle whatever jobs there are to be my full-time campaign manager. I know she has much energy and enthusiasm and that I am lucky to have her in my team. There is also plenty of support with press and website and simple logistics from party HQ, as I try hard to get my head to where it needs to be. People there are endlessly patient with my requests and my 'not knowing' but I believe they understand it's because I want to do a good job, even if we are pretty much last into the field from a standing start. We have, however, lost our director of elections, Kevin Cunningham, who simply had too much on his plate.

We have tea and go to the Wyatt for the launch of the local councillors' campaign. Keith Martin is the sitting Labour county and borough councillor and David Fallon has joined him on the ticket. It's a good meeting. I talk a lot about community and building on what we have, although I'm not sure I'm striking the right note yet. It's very difficult to know what to say about Europe that matters. I think I need a bit of research, something to give me a hook. Someone tells me today that I have already made my mark, that I am a footnote to history and that's something to be proud of, that they would like to stand up for what they believe in and that it takes courage to do it. I say it's easy when you're right. A man at the meeting points out simple things that are wrong, such as the lack of wheelchair access to the tourist office in Westport.

We have tea and sandwiches. We are so hungry we could eat the table. It reminds me of cornflakes at midnight in Weston-super-Mare! I was directing a film for BBC One called *Killer in the Family*, which was a series of interviews with people in that situation, including John Sutcliffe, father of the Yorkshire Ripper. One woman had a son, who at the age of twenty-one, had raped and murdered an eighteen-year-old woman. She was distraught and her life had effectively been destroyed by what had happened. We had been talking to her for a long time about doing an interview and she finally agreed. We knew how vulnerable she was so we took our time – actually nine hours in the end because she would lose her train of thought sometimes and we would stop for her to have a break, then start again. When we got back to our hotel at two in the morning we were starving. In true budget-cutting style we were in a small hotel with no room service. We'd hardly eaten all day so we quite literally raided the breakfast room and the team and crew had cornflakes!

Making that film was unusual for another thing to do with food. It was the only time in my seventeen years of television that someone cooked us a meal. She was Betty Scott, mother of Denis Nilsen, who until the conviction of Harold Shipman in 2000 had the dubious honour of being Britain's biggest serial killer, having killed and dismembered sixteen young men. (The Shipman Enquiry in 2002 concluded that Shipman had probably killed 250 people!) I never forgot Betty's generosity to us: she was a pensioner who was completely bewildered by her son's behaviour, yet she was not so consumed by herself that she could not be kind to us. As we interviewed her, those with keen ears can hear the pot of potatoes boiling, in the pauses when she is gathering herself to speak about the unspeakable.

I've stayed in the Westport Plaza's sister hotel, the Castlecourt, before so I had hoped to talk to the co-owner Anne Corcoran but it doesn't happen as we are late back. Over sandwiches, Mags and I try to brainstorm something I can do on the campaign that has a purpose wherever I go – but it's not working. Our brains are exhausted; it's been one very long day. Time for bed. Fab big bed. Instant sleep.

Tea tally: 5

Wednesday 22 April

Up at 5.30. Breakfast in the foyer at 6am and on the road. We make good time on a glorious morning, stopping for tea! We get to Buswells with plenty of time to spare, which is just as well because the duck T-shirts have gone astray! Mags gets on the phone to chase them. Soon after my sister Anne arrives with my children, who travelled up on the train last night. They're very excited about the occasion and have never been in Buswells or at a press conference. Nessa Childers arrives and we have a cup of tea together. We reflect on whether it's a good thing to include children or not: we have each chosen the opposite course. Mags does my make-up in the ladies and Ombudsman Emily O'Reilly comes in so we shake hands and she wishes me well. People always imagine – largely from movies I think – that toilets are places for skulduggery, double-dealing, drugs and murder. In our case we haven't seen each other for years and we remark on how time has brought both of us journalists to such different positions.

All the MEPs are here now and we meet with Eamon and the party press officer, Tony Heffernan, who tell us what the format is. I will speak first after Eamon. As ever, we are told to be brief. We walk down the road to the EU office on the corner of Molesworth Street and have our pictures taken carrying our own official election posters. It's quite weird but fortunately the photo of me is OK so I'm not too embarrassed. At least it doesn't make me look like a witch.

Just before I get up to speak, I realise my heart is literally pounding. It's not very often that happens and I'm not sure why. I guess it's because I'm speaking to the press, which I haven't done before, apart from the first day when the event was a blur. The kids are wearing the T-shirts – 'Dad's at home minding the ducks' – 'Vote Susan O'Keeffe'. I start by showing the photo of my eldest daughter, Roberta, in my arms after my trial. I say that it's been fourteen years since that event and little has changed in Irish political life in that time and that's why I'm going into politics. To explain how communities share in times of plenty, my children give a box of duck eggs to each candidate and to Eamon and I talk about the importance of community and sharing. Does it work? Who knows…Eamon responds by saying he has inspected the eggs and they are suitably dirty. The Munster candidate, Alan Kelly, says something similar. Nessa doesn't mention them and Proinsias de Rossa says he was a snotty-nosed kid who grew up in inner-city Dublin so he doesn't know that stuff.

There's an unexpected lesson for me which I must try to put to more serious effect: setting the agenda or at least forcing a response from people, that they feel they have to say something about it, that they can't ignore it. The speeches are made, then questions. There are none for the candidates, only for Eamon and Proinsias. It's really interesting to try to make an impact and to be ignored because we are merely 'wannabes' with no authority at all. Nothing like a press conference to remind you of that! I'm glad it's over, though, as I feel well and truly launched now and want to stop talking about why I got into politics and instead about what matters to people and why they should vote Labour.

Kay and Des Murray, my mother and father-in-law, came and I'm grateful they did. There's a lovely photo of Kay – a profile picture with my poster behind. I'd really like to see one of the kids. They were well behaved and patient with the whole thing and they didn't give me grief – well not much – about the T-shirts.

I've promised that there will be no more tricks and there won't!

We go on to Leinster House. The candidates and campaign managers meet for sandwiches and tea. It's useful to chat. Alan says vehicles with branding are good to park in places, like a mobile poster. Maybe I could persuade a few people to do it for me. We talk about Libertas. It's really not having an effect anywhere except the North-West, but I guess that's what I expected. It's Ganley, not Libertas. I hadn't realised that Libertas wasn't registered as a party but for the life of me, don't know why that might be. I guess all the candidates won't meet together again, which seems very odd indeed – to be sharing the same stresses and strains but to be completely separate somehow. Alan was amusing, talking about places he can't go back to because they're sick of the sight of him – if only! Proinsias reminded us that crime matters. His campaign is called 'Jobs and Justice' and he offers that slogan to all of us if we want to use it.

Mark Garrett and David Leach, the national election organiser, talk about Labour Party campaigns often being lost in the last week when people lose momentum, lose sight of the finishing line and possibly run out of money. They say we should put aside money and have a vague plan to be doing something different in the last week to get us over the line. Ah, if only there *was* money to set aside. Millionaire politics this isn't! I sense also a bit of politics at the table, a bit of rivalry between certain party members, but I like not knowing about all that because then I'd start judging and taking sides. That would be a distraction for me at this point as I have quite enough to get my head round

I say goodbye to Kay and Des and walk the kids to the station for the train. They're tired but they say it was good. They are very sweet about my speech and Roberta notices that I was the only candidate without notes and how that makes a difference. Perhaps it's not wise to do that but I find notes hard to incorporate. I used notes yesterday and felt uneasy about it. I realise that speaking without notes is not something everyone can do. We were encouraged into public speaking at school, aged nine! I remember winning a prize for giving a talk about bamboo when I was ten. I've no idea to this day why I chose bamboo but the idea of standing up in front of 120 other children and speaking… well it has certainly helped. I notice too that Eamon never uses notes and completely commands his audience without them. It's in sharp contrast to British and American politicians who rarely if ever leave the safety of the autocue, such is the management of each and every word. We have not yet arrived at that point but I'm sure it is only a matter of time.

I discover that *News at One* on RTÉ used a bit of everyone's speech. They used the eggs for mine but will it matter? Will it make people smile? Will they remember! Will they care? Most people have background noise for politics so won't have clocked it at all. RTÉ's political correspondent, Brian Dowling, makes the point that it will be difficult for me to get elected because I have no experience of politics. It makes me wonder what you really need to be good at this job? The art of being a politician? Being good at reading, understanding, questioning, absorbing? Yes, yes, yes – I know the answer already. But at least I can offer an option to people and that's democracy: they get to choose.

Emails and a press strategy meeting with Paul Daly. We discuss strategy for the next while, what to concentrate on, whether to come out and attack or wait and be well behaved. Is Ganley some kind of touchstone in the constituency? Probably. We watch the news at six o'clock. There are shots of us walking down the street with the posters, a bit of Eamon, a name-check of all of us. I'm not frowning or nodding: that's progress.

I have an off-radar meeting with a friendly person who provides some useful advice about the big targets to try to hit. No surprises: education, third-level fees, farming, the HSE squeeze, cancer services, being positive about Lisbon, I should avoid pro-life debate and is this time to talk about social justice? It is useful for its clarity. My friend K then talks about helping out in Donegal, which would be great. Because we came in so late I'm relying on goodwill, which, I'm beginning to find, abounds.

It's been a long day: time to stop.

Tea tally: 7

Thursday 23 April

I work today so no politics: but that's not really true. I'm disappointed not to find a pic of the girls in any paper – that's a shame. *The Irish Times* reports that I gave out eggs and shows a photo from after the trial but without the context for either it is meaningless and quite silly. The photo they use is of us struggling with our posters. I am to the fore with a very serious face (I need a face transplant) but with my poster quite strategically at the front so that's good, apparently.

I'm feeling a bit blue today. It's all too difficult and not helped by a very dark day, cold and wet. After yesterday, that's a shock. I'm having my doubts all over again about the game of politics, about what I need to learn, about whether the duck stunt was a good stunt or not. I discover that Alan Kelly wanted to hand out jerseys but wasn't allowed so I think he was a bit fed up that I got away with my stunt. We just went ahead and did it without telling anyone but was it the right thing to do? Does this game force you into a strait-jacket? If so, I will have trouble finding one to fit as my instinct is always to break free of them. I talk to some friends who are great for encouraging me and reminding me that I really can't lose.

One strange thing is that the election has totally displaced the day-to-day survival stuff of freelance work. It's only for a couple of months and I'm not really planning beyond June as it's just too difficult to do that. Not because I might be in Brussels, although it's remotely possible, but because I don't know what politics will mean then and how it will it affect my career? That's too big a question to ponder for now so instead I have a quick scan of the underground pylon campaign literature from the North-East Pylon Pressure Group. What they say seems to make sense on paper: put the interconnector underground rather than using high-voltage overhead power lines and don't rely on outmoded technology.

Tea tally: 3

Friday 24 April
I drive to Galway to the launch of the campaign of local candidate Derek Nolan. Mags can't come and I feel a little lost. A big crowd has gathered in the Menlo Park Hotel and I am introduced to many people, all of whom are warm and welcoming. But I'm tired and in the end I ask if the speeches can start! For some reason, when it comes to mine, I feel like crying as I manage to express some of the anger I feel about what's happening to our country

and how bad things are. Perhaps it's because I'm tired but it certainly comes from the heart. Both Michael D and Derek make good speeches too and it's a good start to the campaign in Galway. A quick drink and it's bed for me.

Tea tally: 6

Monday 28 April

There is something about Mondays, something about the break in rhythm that happens on Sundays. We drive to Letterkenny and endure a long pause before we get going and canvass on the streets. It's not very successful: a lot of people are not interested or they are polite but uninterested or listen to a couple of sentences but do not engage. It feels like alien territory here: Labour in Letterkenny wouldn't be strong. We go door-to-door and that's much better – at least there is dialogue and we have a bit of fun hauling my poster around and introducing it! There is anger on the doorstep – the cliché of the year – but it's real: nurses, teachers, Gardaí, parents. These are people in nice new houses who would not be too badly off but who have mortgages and are looking at their bills and wondering, as their wages fall, how they will cope. It's a lovely evening and there are lots of people around. I'm with local council candidate Siobhan McLaughlin and a number of her supporters. It's very good-humoured and we cover a lot of houses.

Siobhan suggests Mags and I stay with her and it's so nice not to be in a hotel but in a real house, complete with open fire. One of the things that she is campaigning about is the possibility that the community services budgets are about to be terminated. It's small money that supports social enterprises in local communities and she firmly believes that Minister Éamon Ó Cuív is considering cutting it.

We spend some time sorting out the detritus of the day. There is a lot of it: various requests from constituencies, organisations and the party, emails and meetings. We agree that my local media coverage has to be heightened and that tomorrow I must aim to get on Highland Radio with something relevant. There and then I write a letter to Shaun Doherty, who hosts a very good show every weekday. It reflects the evening of canvassing which, when you think of how these experiences are multiplied across the country, makes you realise how bad things are on the ground, behind closed doors.

Tea tally: 8

28 April 2009

Dear Shaun

Just as well I'm running for the Labour Party or I'd have ended up in Letterkenny General last night with a bloody nose!

That's how cross people are on the doorstep here: when we rang the doorbell, one man opened it and said it was just as well we weren't Fianna Fáil or he'd have given us a bloody nose. Given that he was over sixty-five, I don't think he falls into the category of hothead!

People in Letterkenny aren't just cross. They're furious. What was most curious, though, was that people weren't complaining about the hit to their own pocket. That came later. No, first, they were upset about the way in which the government has managed to continue paying itself good salaries and pensions or – in some cases – two pensions. They were furious that Fianna Fáil had not stuck to the cutbacks in TDs' pay that it said would happen in the budget. One woman, Marita Sharkey, wanted to ask Brian Cowen a very simple question: why does he, Brian, believe he should earn more than Barack Obama?

To be honest, I'm not often stumped for an answer but I was to that one! And what of the man who's looking at his children playing in the garden on a lovely sunny evening, wondering how he will manage on five hundred euro less every month. He doesn't want to think about the next budget. Will the five go up to six? Or more?

Then there's the care worker whose contract runs out in a few weeks' time, terrified she will lose her job and also worried that if she's not replaced, who will do her work. She's kept busy forty hours a week and she says these are frontline services that are being hit, right here in Letterkenny.

And there is class size too: too many children and not enough teachers. This comes from both teachers and parents. Their disbelief is tangible. How could kids be first in the line to take the hit in these cutbacks. That's what they want to know, although they know perfectly well there's no answer from a government that is not listening and is completely out of touch.

I don't even think we got round to the fact that lots of children are being taught in temporary prefabs with no prospect at all of a proper school with decent facilities and the sense of pride that comes with all that, that allows schools to become the cornerstone of their communities.

Nor did we get to cancer services being moved to Galway or the state of the roads or the lack of broadband but as we were finishing our canvass, we met one man who smiled and said that our arrival on his doorstep marked the 'beginning of the last days for Fianna Fáil'.

Tuesday 27 April

Today was a day of madness. From a local newspaper interview in Letterkenny, to the absence of a rape trauma centre, to the funding for Breastcheck being pulled and going on Highland Radio to talk about that, to a big welcome and lunch at the ICTU centre to a shake-hands in the SIPTU centre and the Women's Co-op, then a bit of background research on water basin management, to a meeting with the IFA about the potential of forestry and the damage being done by supermarkets, to Coastwatch and its campaign to protect the native oyster from the imported Japanese one. And it's not over yet. A bit of pushing and pulling about Breastcheck in Leitrim and Clare and a meeting to launch Shay Carbin's council campaign in Donegal town with a few ham sandwiches and a cup of tea and a very warm reception, even though many people in the room were obviously not rose-wearers. It was the kind of day that is made of mini-triumphs amid the chaos and that shows how hard it is to be organised when you're rushing and reacting. But it does remind me how much I enjoy meeting people in the places they work and listening to their stories, even if it's mostly about what is wrong and what they're short of and how it could be better. I find I enjoy the challenge of switching from subject to subject and am grateful for all those years of research on such a wide range of subjects. It's a bit like a mad day on the newsdesk but there is always something to connect with and some link for a question or occasionally a piece of advice from a previous life.

The mood music is very strong for Labour so it is all the more important to be very cautious. People are talking about change but they have to change in the polling booth for it to matter. Will they get out on the streets and vote? Mary Coughlan's name is mentioned, not very favourably. Some people are embarrassed, others are furious and nobody seems to buy the Taoiseach's endorsement of her. If I'm not mistaken, this is her constituency.

A and K come to offer help in any way they can. That would be great. I don't know how it will work but we'll see. I think it's quite hard to volunteer when you have a life and this isn't part of it and you don't know what it will mean. It's a bit like me deciding to run.

We stay in Ard na Breatha guesthouse, which has the EU flower symbol for adhering to certain environmental criteria. They are also part of the Green Box movement encouraging eco-tourism – 'responsible escapism', I call it. That's why we've chosen it: to support eco-tourism as a venture in Ireland. I think it's one area of tourism that will grow and that Ireland is well placed to take advantage of because we are still a comparatively clean country. Germany and Norway are the lead countries when it comes to this kind of environmental approach The quiet and calm atmosphere here is just what I need and it's good to get away from more impersonal hotels once in a while (and there's home-made brown bread).

Beginning to enjoy the Twittering. Neil Ward, Labour's Youth Officer in head office, says I've got it now with the 'Donegal women have no breasts' line. It's a good one but can I repeat it?? Twittering is good for concentrating the mind and the message. The limit of 143 characters is possibly someone's idea of a joke but without it I wouldn't have come up with that line and it does sum up the government's attitude to women and to breast cancer.

Will I invite John Podesta to speak? Would he come in such a short space of time? As the saying goes in journalism: 'If you don't ask, you don't get.' Will he remember me? Podesta was Bill Clinton's chief of staff at the White House and more recently he headed Barack Obama's transition team for the White House. In 2003 and 2004 I made two programmes for BBC TV called *The Situation Room*. The idea was a model on the real Situation Room in the White House where the big hitters in the White House administration go if there is a crisis – usually a foreign policy/terrorist crisis. We invited men and women who had once been in the Situation Room themselves in their real job. We had players from the CIA, the State Department, the Defense Department, the Armed Forces and so on, and we devised a crisis for them to play out on camera: Pakistan and India on the verge of war – close to reality, rooted in reality but entirely faked. Podesta played himself and really got stuck in, complete with his trademark can of Coke. He's a good, sharp guy so I think he *will* remember. I know that after we recorded the first one, they shook hands at the end and thanked me and said they, 'Didn't know how I had pulled it off but it felt real.' They really enjoyed it. You could tell they were engrossed and Podesta, in particular, loved trying to work out where the storyline was going. They had never done anything like it before for television, so we all really enjoyed it.

Tea tally: 10 (That's a record.)

Wednesday 29 April

We go to Shay's office in Donegal town and take silly pictures outside it with posters. Then to his family office where they're working hard, then out to a lovely man called Hugh McNamee who is at home with his two boys and who has trained to make chocolate – Velure – from a small custom-built kitchen. He's good at it too: the chocolates are delicious and I admire him for getting up and sorting out something that fits into his lifestyle. He still gets to help with the care of his children and he supplies businesses locally with a view to doing a bit more when the children get older. It's always good to meet people who are doing. Then off to the local hospital with its brand new X-ray centre which still hasn't opened. We meet some of the older people coming to the drop-in centre. They are so delightful – warm, happy to chat, smiling and so grateful for someone to take care of them. The soup smells good and the place seems well run with a genuine sense of care for these people. I get to meet the manager and explain what I'm trying to do.

We pass the office of Tánaiste Mary Coughlan. She's in the news today because her minister of state, John McGuinness, who was one of the seven junior ministers demoted earlier in the week by the Taoiseach, has been very critical of the leadership of the party and there have been reports of rows between him and Mary Coughlan. Most of us were extremely confused by the idea that these ministers who lost their jobs would receive a severance payment of €53,000. Health Minister Mary Harney is promising today that by the end of 2009 Ireland will be one of the top three countries 'in the world' for breast cancer services. Try telling that to the people in the North-West, who've been campaigning to keep the breast cancer service in Sligo so that patients don't have to travel long distances when they're ill. It's a hostage to fortune for the minister.

Then it's a quick goodbye and off again – to Cavan – to the opening of Liam Hogan's office. He's a first-time Labour candidate too and he is there with his father and Des Cullen, the sitting Labour councillor. It's really nice. They've made a fuss. I get to cut the ribbon and declare it open. Then we make a few speeches. I cheat and nick two roses from the vase and give one to each of the two candidates. They give me a Cavan crystal vase with two roses in it. We have tea and sandwiches and I talk to Liam's dad, who is a long-time party member and recounts funny stories from previous campaigns. Then off again to Carrickmacross to the launch of Peadar's Markey's campaign for the local council elections. I bump into George Clooney too and Twitter that George is supporting my campaign – well, the cardboard George is! I am beginning to realise that campaigning would be impossible without good, friendly central hotels where staff are always happy to serve us tea and let us plug in laptops and mobiles. Before we leave Cavan Crystal Hotel we meet a delegation from the Monaghan hospital campaign in the lobby.

The problem is that the HSE can't keep lots of small hospitals open but they can't close them either when the road between Cavan and Monaghan is poor and consultants won't travel it and ambulances get lost. An elderly woman is kept in Cavan half the night, then they call a cab to take her home (costing her €80) and a man ends up trying to walk home from Cavan to Monaghan, half-dazed, in the middle of the night. This is the Irish health service in the 21st century. I know I've heard it all before but I'm still shocked and, as ever, it is in rural areas that the problems are most acute. The big cities are pretty well served but go beyond a certain distance and you are forced to travel. This would be fine if the roads were good or there were sufficient ambulances or excellent public transport but there isn't. Making the centralisation argument doesn't work if the infrastructure is inadequate.

I put out a statement about the elderly community scheme being suspended. Even though I am raising the subject a lot, I fear it will not make any difference. It's such a small sum of money compared with the amount that is wasted on unnecessary things.

Statement by Susan O'Keeffe, Labour's North-West Euro Election Candidate

Wednesday 29 April 2009

The Scheme of Community Support for Older People involves the whole community. Local voluntary groups install monitored alarms and door and window locks for older people in their community. Not only does the scheme provide important protection and security for elderly people, it brings the community together, and no government, no matter how miserly, can put a price on that.

This is just another sign of a wider attack on the fabric of our communities. In relation to hospitals,

Garda stations and other vital services, there is a real danger that the government will introduce cutbacks over the coming months that will tear the heart out of local communities. It is a stupid strategy that will cause untold damage. Our communities will be vital, as Ireland tries to lift itself out of the current recession. Now, more than ever, we have to ensure that vital health and welfare services in Cavan, Monaghan and throughout the north-east are maintained.

Time to head for Peadar Markey's launch in Callan's Pub in Carrickmacross. The pub is a time-warp, a lot of old left-wing hangers-on from all over the place mixed with a healthy handful of young recently-joined Labour members and quite a few women. They too are very kind and give me a GAA shirt from the local club, Donaghmore. Apparently they couldn't decide whether or not to give it to me because they're worried I mightn't like it. I love it and put it on immediately and have my picture taken. They're a nice bunch and we have more tea and sandwiches. We make speeches and chat, then at about 10 o'clock, it's time – *not* for bed but to head for Dublin. What a long day. In bed, I write a press release about the cancer services; I'm pretty angry.

Fianna Fáil's Border of Death

Your chances of surviving breast cancer are lower once you cross Fianna Fáil's border of death.

It's that simple. From Dublin to Galway, a line has been drawn. And north of that line has been abandoned.

What is going on in Mary Harney's office? What is going on in Professor Drumm's head?

Where is the Taoiseach?

And why is Mary Coughlan, Tánaiste, woman and Fianna Fáil TD north of the border of death, not beating the table on behalf of her constituents

So just in case you four are not sure what's going on or you've gone deaf or you haven't managed to read any of the statistics relating to the North-West and cancer incidence and in case you've never had cancer and been bundled onto a bus in Moville to endure a rocky journey to Galway for treatment, let me just remind you – all four of you – what you've done.

You have drawn a line of death across our country. And you've walked away and said 'good job'.

Those people who die or die earlier will die because of what you have done.

Those people who will struggle in the back of a bus to survive the journey, never mind cope with cancer and difficult treatment, will struggle because of what you have done.

Those nurses and doctors stressed to the hilt trying to cope are stressed because of what you have done.

You don't care. It's that simple.

And we know you don't. Because, if you cared, this wouldn't happen.

Ever.

Tea tally: 8

Thursday 30 April

The OECD report says the recession is worse in Ireland than anywhere else.

I work today – now there's a novelty – training people on ideas-pitching and brainstorming. It's good and I enjoy it but oh my God when I walk up Ely Place for a meeting at Labour Party HQ, there is my face all over a car. Now that is truly peculiar. To laugh or cry? You have to see the funny side of it and I do. Then within a moment, it's back to the hard work; sending emails, reading policy documents and checking that the diary is up to date. There is always a lot to absorb: not just the detail of what things are called and where they're based and who runs them but a sense of what they are and what they do and how they fit into a million other systems too. Europe is awash with organisations and associations and sub-committees and funds and there are hundreds of other organisations based in Europe to try to keep up with the official ones. It's almost like two parallel universes of bureaucracy, one pushing paper in and the other pushing it out.

I do it. I invite John Podesta. I speak to his press guy at the Center. He says it probably won't happen because of the time-frame but he says send the mail anyway. It's a very long day before we get back home to Sligo but that's where we need to be for the morning. We load ourselves into the new car, hoping that no one is looking. I am warned not to roll down the back window unless I want my face to roll up and disappear. We only have it half an hour and already it feels full of campaign stuff. I felt I did three days work today: I probably did!

Tea tally: 2 (That's better.)

Friday 1 May

Mayday – Labour Day – but we don't celebrate that. It seems odd for the Labour Party not to but we're too busy anyway. We start in Crossmolina at a meeting about the Western Rail Corridor. For the life of me I can't work out why they're having this meeting. The only issue about this project is whether the government will ever pay for more than the first quarter of it. Transport Minister Noel Dempsey comes to say how wonderful it all is and how much he cares about it, then reveals that the only money available is for a report on phase II and III. He adds that the idea of phase II and III will only be implemented if phase I is successful, which phase I is unlikely to be because it's the least busy part of the route. So I get up and introduce myself and ask if, given that the Minister for Finance made no pledge to the project in the budget and that the capital spending in transport has been cut by a significant amount, he could now make a pledge that the project would proceed. I am right at the back of the room so I really feel I am making a point in standing up but it seems to me that no one else in the room is going to ask the question. In response, Noel Dempsey pretty much says that only the stupid could misunderstand his speech and his commitment. Quite! Afterwards, there was tea and coffee and many people came over to say quietly in my ear that mine was the only true question to be asked and that the minister should not have been so rude: it's so ignorant and stupid to be rude when he didn't have to be. It was interesting.

I did my first interview as Gaeilge. We had to stop at least three times when I forgot the words but the interviewer was generous enough to say my Irish was good, which it would be if I practised. I did a couple of other interviews too but Midwest Radio news didn't use any clips at lunch – just a long interview with the minister. *C'est la vie*. A candidate is just that – a wannabee – and getting press is hard work, even when it's clear the government is spinning. The government is the government and this is Mayo, strong Fianna Fáil country.

I talk to my old friend D this morning. He's a good head and says, 'Always ask for the Number One, not just for support,' and that it's often the case that whoever asks first is the person they vote for. I try it out in Claremorris with an elderly man who magically says exactly that: 'You asked me first so I'll vote for you.' If only it were always that easy! D has canvassed for years with Fine Gael so I suspect he knows a thing or two.

We drive back to Sligo, stopping on the way to Knock and taking a few photos, including one of me standing next to a sign that says 'Confessions/Counselling.' Seemed appropriate. We take photographs in Sligo too, of me holding the rugby Grand Slam trophies – another Twitter moment. The trophies are on tour and the O2 shop is crowded, mostly with men. Someone I know introduces me to two elderly FF supporters who complain bitterly about the party and say they will vote for me.

Then it's up to Sligo Grammar to talk to Transition Year pupils – a hard task on a Friday afternoon and harder still because it's my daughter's class. I talk about corruption, without slagging off the government. Instead I am critical of all governments and all those in power. There are some interesting questions afterwards. We take some silly pictures of the girls with the van which, needless to remark, is a cause of much laughter. We have christened it Sue Force and are disappointed when, just outside the school, it suddenly starts spewing smoke and smelling of burning. Not so hot for a brand-new car! My friend, Edison Whiteside from Riverside Motors in Collooney, comes to the rescue but can find nothing wrong so we press on to Galway in time for most of the Galway United match.

I sit next to Michael D, who is club president, and they beat St Pats 2-1, which is good news. He is such an ardent supporter and it's a side to him I simply didn't know so I am honoured to be there with him. Fortunately he's not the type to try a running commentary with me, probably realising that much of it would be wasted. I quite like soccer but I'm not very good on the detail of who plays for whom and where they played before. I'm just happy to watch the performance. The best bit is always the half-time tea which we enjoy, as the weather is quite cold. There isn't a huge crowd, which I guess is a sign of the times.

The new unemployment figures came out today: they're terrible. I think people have given up predicting where they might go next: all we see now are lengthening queues at the dole office. I would have thought it was fairly easy to predict such figures in a country this size but there are real predictions and political predictions. They bear no similarity to one another. I don't hold with this not telling the truth, not allowing people to understand what's happening. It's a bit like the old-fashioned doctor-patient relationship: the doctor decided what to do and never told the patient that he had two days left to live. This massaging of figures before they come out is unforgivable. I still do not believe this government's argument that they did not know the crash was coming or that it would be quite so bad. *I* knew and if I knew, they must have known. When I say 'I knew', I meant that I knew enough from the signs in the US, the UK and here that things were about to take a serious hit and that people were over-borrowed and over-paid. And the evidence that proves that I knew: I rearranged my life entirely to get rid of my mortgage and my debt! It wasn't that the FF government didn't know: they just chose not to say.

We go from the football to the dogs – quite literally. There's a Labour Party night and we're in time to see the winner of the big race, appropriately called 'Bred to Win'. I enjoy those photos. Being photographed with a greyhound winner may be the high point of the campaign. The owners are from Cork so that's great. I can't canvass them; I can just be me. The councillors allow me to make the presentation, which is kind of them. I press the flesh of loads of people afterwards. It's hard work when they're on a night out but most people are nice. And the redoubtable Sabina is here in support.

Tea tally: 5

Saturday 2 May
We go canvassing at a shopping centre in Galway. It's a lovely morning and there are quite a lot of people out. It's interesting: most people are supportive. Some don't stop, some are very angry, some talk about having to buy cut-price meat, losing thousands on investments or having to pay a pension levy on a non-existent pension – there is huge unhappiness. After Galway, we drive to Glenties, which is a fair way. For once we eat dinner and calculate that it might be the first dinner all week. Then we go to the parish church at Ardara, where the Cup of Tae Music Festival is on. We shake hands with locals coming out the gate and I almost climb into a tractor to shake one man's hand. In the main they are polite, although some are clearly *not* Labour supporters. We go to one

of the pubs, the Corner House Bar, and listen to some nice music for a while. The owner says business is good and he plays a lot of music himself. There's a great atmosphere and the music is first-class. I've never been in Ardara before but it's a really pretty town. It's good to get the chance to enjoy a place and some music and switch off for a few minutes. I drive the car back to Sligo. Mags is not feeling well, probably a consequence of too many long days.

The downside of Ivana Bacik's decision to run for Dublin Central in the by-election resulting from Tony Gregory's death is that I will lose Paul Daly, who has been my busy PR team. I recognise that it makes sense and lucky Ivana; I'm really pleased she's running. She is a good strong candidate. We will have to fall back on our own resources for the moment.

Tea tally: 5

Sunday 3 May

Sadly, my first exposure to pure rudeness is in Sligo. We start canvassing outside the cathedral. That's quite good. People are OK and some are keen to find that I live locally or that I know about the Sligo cancer services. Some people just walk by but that's fine. We move to Dunnes in Cranmore and a handful of people are rude. They take the leaflet and throw it in front of me or just glare. A polite no would be fine really: I respect people's views. I just can't bear rudeness but I guess I'd better start learning that I am not entitled to manners. In a way I'm glad because I have been saying all along that people were too nice and you end up thinking the whole world is supporting you when clearly this is not true. So a reality check is good news if not very nice.

We move on to the races and that's even worse! I suspect that it's not a great haunt for Labour supporters. Even the cops give us grief about driving my car round the streets at the same time as Paschal Mooney's car is going around. We see Paschal. He doesn't stop to shake any hands outside but goes straight through into the grounds. I opt not to go in. People don't want to be canvassed when they're out for the day – it's not right. Marian Harkin's supporters turn out too. We have a chat and they say that they are quite concerned about Declan Ganley's impact and how much money he is spending on advertising. That would be hard to miss as his posters are quite literally everywhere. Even if you wanted a poster site now you would be hard pushed to get one. And it's legal. Paid advertising can go up any time. Unpaid – i.e. posters stuck to telegraph poles – can only go up from 5 May, although there's the usual row in some places, because people are cheating and going up early. I've seen quite a few around here – it's to steal the best spots.

I get a nice text from Neil Ward to say that the Irish blogger of the year is enjoying my Twittering and my sense of humour. That's encouraging; one skill I have learned from campaigning is Twittering! Now how can I use that to enhance my life? Answers – polite – in a Twitter please!

Tea tally: 3

Monday 4 May

My soap box is under construction – hurrah! Otherwise it's a miserable morning here. We parked the car in Coolaney overnight: it's what I call 'silent canvassing'. If only we had a car in each county. They are probably the best value for money in terms of advertising. My friend A comes by and reminds me that the local papers will not cover us at all unless we buy advertising! So much for the free press: many are just advertisement sheets really. I knew that but it is confirmed to me now and it saddens me because it makes clear how badly local communities are served in terms of news or information. We go out to Rosses Point to cheer on the walkers and runners who are out for the Carers' Association. There's a big turn-out so we cheer and do our best to encourage them as it's a 10k distance and quite cold and windy. We shake hands at the end, too, and I'm really impressed with the enthusiasm of the participants.

Then a quick cuppa and on to the Showgrounds where I have no loyalty, as it's Finn Harps (Donegal) and Sligo Rovers. Well, no public loyalties. People are more welcoming here than at the races. One man has quite an argument with me about Ruairi Quinn's financial policies of old and gives me grief for not agreeing with him. A couple going in dismiss all politicians out of hand. I try to debate it with the husband but his wife is having none of it and ushers him and the kids along in a hurry. It's quite hard, really: people just want a day out and don't want to be hassled. But how else can you find them and try to reach out to them? If we stayed home and didn't try, we would be accused of being lazy and not caring.

Mags and I have a meeting afterwards and try to sort out some of the hurdles for the coming week. It's turning hectic. And the posters have turned up; soon they will be on poles and bridges and roundabouts all round the west of Ireland. I've had a reply from Podesta's office: predictably, it's a no. Nothing ventured, nothing gained. I resolve to put something up on the website about him and *The Situation Room* programmes.

More importantly I have written the fundraising letter. It was never going to be easy to ask people you know to fund your political career. Yet, in this country, and most others, there is no other way and it's accepted. I'm sure there are plenty of people who would have no problem asking but I have had to steel myself to do it. Over the years I have always had the habit of *not* asking friends for information about stories even when they were well-placed to help. This was because I was once accused of asking a civil servant who was a friend for information on a very sensitive story. I had not done so but no one believed me. I determined then never to ask so that I could always stand by my integrity. Asking for money as I do in this letter seems slightly in the same bracket:

> That's it – I really have gone into politics – not because of the posters or the speeches or the campaigning. It's the make-up!
>
> Given that you know me as well as you do, you can have a bit of a laugh at my expense: the woman who went through almost her whole life without even a make-up bag, now won't leave home without it! Yes, it comes to all of us in the end – the need to look just that bit better than reality.
>
> I don't mind if it means that people might stop and listen for ten seconds longer. I don't mind if it makes the message that bit easier to give, but I do enjoy the days when I don't have to wear it. The campaigning's a real challenge: vying for people's time when they're putting kids to bed or shopping or having their hair cut or sitting in their taxis.

That's why I'm writing to you – sure you knew anyway – but I need to raise some money to keep campaigning. It's the little things – cups of tea, newspapers, petrol, a cheese sandwich, then the bigger things – some posters, newspaper advertising, leaflets. It all adds up and since I'm not into 'millionaire politics', I'm hoping that small individual donations will add up to enough to keep me on the road for the next four weeks. It's not that long but it will be intense and constant and it's a huge constituency – the four provinces of Ireland and around 960,000 people!

Any amount you can give would be wonderful. Twenty euro will buy us a few hundred miles of petrol; fifty euro will keep us going for a day…it all adds up… and more than that would be wonderful. A guy on the doorstep tonight was all set to give me a bloody nose – to use his words – because he thought I was from Fianna Fáil. People really are angry. I know you're not in my constituency but you know that this is about getting people elected across the country and sending a message to the government. The Labour Party is less well organised here so we need all the help we can get.

There – I've done it. It's not easy to ask friends for donations, even though I'm reliably informed that Hillary Clinton spent one-third of her time asking for money. No, no, that doesn't mean I'll be back pestering you again. I won't. This is a once-off request. I know that times are hard and you know I'll understand if this is a stretch beyond your limit.

And it will go to my campaign. There are lots of candidates running for the Labour Party at European and local election but everyone raises funds for their own campaign. What I'd really like is to have something to spend in the last two weeks of the campaign when it's hard to keep going and you need fresh momentum and a fresh message.

Thanks for reading this. Thanks for your messages of support so far. They really have helped. I just felt it was time to stand up and try to do something concrete; to offer to get out there and work for our country, for all of us. Politics is a strange place and it has plenty of flaws but it's the way we come together to do business; it's the only way we've got so we just have to make a bigger effort to make it better.

Tea tally: 3

Tuesday 5 May

Time to do the girl thing and go shopping. As the Sligo meeting with the party leader is on Thursday I'd better find something to wear. Mags insists so off we go and Roberta comes at school lunchtime and manages to get a smoothie out of me because I'm so distracted. She is there for the final vetting purposes. We do well and manage in a moment of madness to buy two dresses. Now here I have to confess that a certain amount of coercion was called for; it really became a two-against-one scenario, a 'try it on or else' moment. I don't know that there was a valid 'or else' in the sentence but I knew I wasn't leaving the shop without putting

The Sligo candidates and Eamon Gilmore accompany me to the official signing of my nomination papers at Sligo Courthouse: from left, Jimmy McGarry, Mary Dolan McLoughlin, Marcella McGarry, Alwyn Love and Veronica Cawley.

Driving myself!

Galway council candidates, from left, Derek Nolan, Billy Cameron and Niall McNelis, accompany Proinsias de Rossa and me as we launch the Safer Streets initiative in Galway.

Employing my children to hand out free-range duck eggs at the official launch of all the Labour Party Euro candidates, here with party leader Eamon Gilmore.

Mags Murphy and I share a joke after the launch of the little red dress, aka the candidate, in Sligo.

The heavens open for 'The Siege of Ennis'.

Above left: Roberta's friends enjoy the photo op with the candidate: from left, Roberta, Ali, Ellen, Lesley and Holly.

Above right: The Cancer Bus stops at Sligo General Hospital to a big reception.

Left: The Euro Bus launches its tour of Ireland at the Mercy College in Sligo.

Right: Galway United's president, Michael D, introduces me to Terryland Park.

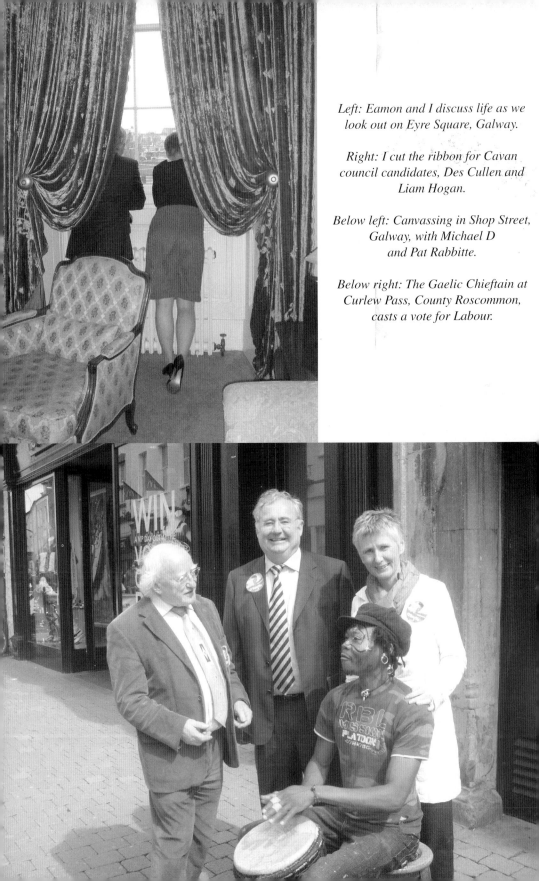

Left: Eamon and I discuss life as we look out on Eyre Square, Galway.

Right: I cut the ribbon for Cavan council candidates, Des Cullen and Liam Hogan.

Below left: Canvassing in Shop Street, Galway, with Michael D and Pat Rabbitte.

Below right: The Gaelic Chieftain at Curlew Pass, County Roscommon, casts a vote for Labour.

I take the floor with Paschal Mooney at the Bealtaine festival in Sligo.

Time to cast the vote: the family flanked by the campaign team, Pat Cooper and Mags.

on the dresses. Oh – and the shoes. Shopping done, then to my hairdresser, Pauline Dineen. We have a small surprise for her – I bring a poster into the shop and show her the first haircut and tell her how well she did and how sorry I am that I couldn't tell her the last time she cut it – the day before I was 'unveiled'. She takes it very well and is delighted, then cuts my hair – short.

There has been so much dispute about my hair and whether it should be short or longer or should have highlights that I still wonder at Hillary Clinton: if she spent one-third of her time fundraising, she must have spent another third getting dressed and manicured. If you're campaigning for the most powerful job in the world, every single moment has to be calculated. But then I guess she never went shopping herself and had someone standing over her saying 'or else'. A woman in public life, no matter what she's standing for, bears so much scrutiny that enormous effort has to be made to consider it in advance. People smile first, then look at what you're wearing! It's hard when you're on the road all the time and we have had to do the odd emergency quick shop.

Jobs done and we move on to the Bealtaine launch in the Sligo Park. Bealtaine is the annual month-long May festival that celebrates the talents and activities of older people. There is a big tea dance in the hotel and it is very well attended, with groups from all over Sligo and North Leitrim. Paschal Mooney is there and he agrees to a waltz; a momentary Fianna Fáil-Labour pact. Let's face it: most of the people in this room have seen every variation on the theme of politics in Ireland and will hardly be anything other than temporarily amused by our effort. And neither of us will be winning a prize for it either but the picture is taken. Paschal is upset at the very real prospect that Pat the Cope Gallagher may be added to the ticket to replace Seán Ó Neachtain. He makes no secret of his annoyance and I am puzzled by how public he is about it: I would have thought that was 'in-house'. Tea with the guests and finally we collapse. I have a million emails to respond to and material to read and a speech to write for tomorrow.

We have our first full-time volunteer, a woman called Pat Cooper, who is currently living in Spain but wants to come and work on our campaign until the end. How great. She concedes at the outset that her family is traditional Fine Gael! I've been invited to attend the Business and Professional Women's Club meeting in the Yeats Building in Sligo. Tonight they have an introduction to creative writing. It's slightly surreal to have tips and practice in creative writing at this juncture but I enjoy it very much and the company is pleasant and welcoming.

Today I get a reply from John Curran's office, telling me that the community support scheme for older people is under review and was suspended 'as part of the effort to stabilise the public finances'. The review will take till September. Perhaps they will review their expenses at the same time.

Tea tally: 7

Thursday 7 May
Phoenix runs a piece saying my tilt at Europe could only mean that I want to run for the Dáil because I haven't a prayer in this constituency and how stupid the Labour Party in Dublin is to be trying to introduce me into the constituency and what a row it will cause if I stand in a general election. I don't know who wrote it or who invented it but they do call me Susan O'Beef so we have a laugh about that. The only thing to do is laugh.

We meet up with the party leader in Longford. By the time we get out at Collooney and Coolaney – right where I live – it's a downpour of enormous proportion. Eamon meets and greets, and in Coolaney, candidate Alwyn Love has the sense to arrange for people to meet in the pub where we're dry.

But on a little red dress day, it hardly matters. We've arrived at the Sligo Park Hotel for the reception. There is time for a quick cup of tea, then it's clothes and make-up. I'm cold and wet but the show must go on. Never in my life have I owned or worn a little red dress so it is a big deal to stand up in a room full of people and make a speech welcoming the party leader wearing such a dress. It seems to entertain a lot of people and those who know me well know to laugh with me, not at me. The speech goes well. It's hard to do that – much harder than I thought – when you know lots of people and the children are there and Grace's friends and people from school and neighbours and the party. Anyway it is well received, then Eamon makes a very good speech. He sticks to the big picture about how we need change, how it's a great country and how the generations to come are relying on us to make the right decisions. I think the fact that we go at it in different ways helps and we neither of us have notes, just mike in hand, which I've found I prefer to the standing mike – that makes me feel like a singer who can't sing.

Eamon and I have a really useful chat with the Sligo Chamber of Commerce, whose main concerns are VAT and cross-border shopping. Eamon suggests that one thing I could talk about is trying, with European support, to have a special trade zone in Ireland which would somehow be able to accommodate the differences in price that are unique to a land border. I wonder how that would work but it sounds interesting. I enjoy getting my teeth into subjects, engaging with people, understanding their concerns.

Then meeting and hand-shaking and thanking people for coming: that's the best part, time to relax and enjoy. It is great to see people come out – it's throwing a party and what if no one comes feeling but that didn't happen – I know head office were concerned that hardly anyone had replied but I had to say that's not the Sligo way – people will come on the day and people will come to hear Eamon Gilmore, the most popular leader in the country. And to be fair, it is a stinker of an evening – the worst rain in Sligo for weeks and that's saying something. Finally a small glass of wine. I am grateful to kick my quite high heels off at the end of the night.

Tea tally: 6

Friday 8 May
D-day, the day for handing in the nomination papers – apparently it has on occasion been forgotten by at least one TD. No papers, no run! I am lucky to have Veronica Cawley, mayor of Sligo, to nominate me and Eamon Gilmore to accompany me, so it makes it feel special. We sign the documents in the office of Kieran McDermott, the returning officer, and he allows us to take some photographs, then a few more outside. Another hurdle on the road. What I never realised before is that all candidates have what's called the 'substitute list', which does exactly what it says on the tin. It seems to cause consternation in some parties – who gets on them and why – but fortunately I have no say in it, nor would I wish to, because that's the politics of politics and, right

now, my energy has to be for the campaign.

On then for a run around Ballina and Crossmolina with Eamon. We meet the local candidates – Harry Barrett and David Moffatt. Eamon really does a speedy canvass – as you have to when you're the leader. He gets such a good reception – everyone knows him and shakes his hand – but we do have a moment with the taxi drivers who say the Labour Party has not stood up for them. Eamon says he has and that the taxi drivers should support Labour and that would solve the problem. The guy in question said he feels dictated to by Eamon, who said that he is just being straight and honest and that the taxis need better regulation. There is quite a number of very angry people – about how cheated they feel and how they're making such a mess and how things are changing. I suggest to Eamon that maybe we should use 'The Times They Are a-Changing' as the anthem because they certainly are and they should know – they've been at this game for a long time. Eamon has been in several different political organisations over the years but he says quite firmly that he thinks it's a seismic change. I hope he's right – the country needs change. Sure, there are people who argue that all politicians are the same, that it makes no difference who is elected. That would be to ignore the enormous damage done by Fianna Fáil in terms of corruption and dishonesty, in terms of the closeness between the government, the bankers and the developers and the general air that this government has governed for some of the people, not all the people. We are now morally bankrupt: our sense of right and wrong has been stolen by a government that makes the rules to suit itself and failed to bring any accountability into the system.

Tea tally: 8

Saturday 9 May

All the days are blurring now because they are so long and so much happens that the beginning and end are hard to find. Today is a bit different, though, as it kicked off with two debates – one on Newstalk and one on Ocean FM in Sligo. It's good to get going. There aren't too many programmes like this so you have to really try hard. Otherwise the Broadcasting Commission of Ireland clock is ticking – whereby stations have to apportion time to candidates depending on their party and status – and it's hard to get on air any other way: although I think I've been on Ocean every day for the past three days! Doing Newstalk meant I was on the phone and not in studio – with Ray O'Malley and MEP Eoin Ryan and the station's political correspondent. I am happy with my performance, managing to interrupt a few times, which is always difficult when not in studio. I expect Ray O'Malley, formerly of the Irish Creamery Milk Suppliers Association, who is running for Libertas, to be really tough on the subject of farming but he isn't.

Then on to Ocean for *Ocean Current* with Paddy Clancy, who has invited first-time candidates to debate. There are Senator Joe O'Reilly of FG, SF's Pádraig Ó Lochlainn and Paschal Mooney, who arrives late enough to be made a fuss of but who has to share a mike with Pádraig. In his day job, Paschal presents a programme for Ocean, so he must have felt just a bit strange in that position. Joe has to talk about Michael McDowell, former PD leader and Minister for Justice, possibly running for FG in a general election because it was reported in the papers today that he had private talks with the party about running. That allows me to say 'old faces old ways' for Fine Gael. Then Paschal has a bit of a moment when he reveals that he will not be happy if Pat the Cope runs and that he is talking to his family about quitting. One gets the impression that he might pull out if that happened – but would he really? Oh goodness, FF people are not happy at the moment. It goes well enough and when the row about Lisbon starts, I sit back and let SF and FF shout at each other.

Then a grab of tea and on to Athlone where it is sunny and we canvass. I get very tired and don't feel well so we have to stop for about half an hour – just yesterday catching up. We go around town with the local Labour Party people and support in general is very good. Lots of people talk to us, lots of smiles, a lot of unhappy FF people – *plus ça change*. It's interesting to feel the way a town is when the councillors are strong. They know the locals well and walk about as if they own it and feel happy shaking hands and introducing me. No wonder FF have done so well over the years, with the councils full of their people and good grass-roots organisation.

Athlone certainly feels like a town that has a lot of potential to go Labour and be as strong as Mullingar. This would be a good axis to build on if they could reach out to Leitrim and Offaly, Biffo country. I imagine he's not sleeping easy these nights. On our way back we have fun with the famous statue of the Gaelic chieftain overlooking wonderful Lough Key – we put the Labour Party folder in with him and I stand next to him. Pity we don't have a ladder to put a Labour hat on him. One must have light moments now and again and good pictures tell another story. I spot a pub called 'The Four Provinces', so out comes the camera. North-West is the only constituency which has counties from all four provinces, which underlines how hard it is to represent it and campaign in it. There are eleven counties with huge variations: from Cavan and Monaghan to Galway and Clare, then Donegal, Mayo, Sligo, Leitrim, Roscommon, Longford and Westmeath, which used to be in Leinster but has been moved. The constituencies are divided on a population basis and the growth of Louth, Meath, Kildare, Carlow, Kilkenny and Wicklow as commuter towns increased the population in Leinster, so Westmeath was sliced off to join North-West. Westmeath people don't feel as if that is their natural hinterland and it isn't! Population-wise, North-West is still the smallest of the four constituencies, with just over 900,000 people. We have an MEP for roughly every 430,000 voters, while the Germans have one for every 850,000. On that basis, we would have just six MEPs.

Sunday 10 May
Glorious, glorious sunny day. Out with Alwyn Love in Coolaney and the An Post cycle for what I call the 'hairy legs' – serious dedicated cyclists. We even meet some from the Burren! Canvassing Clare voters in Sligo seems easy. They are all in good form and enjoying the challenge. I envy them their enthusiasm and their fitness. Then into the launch of the 10k family cycle, also run by An Post. We meet Paschal again and have more photographs. He's still in the dark about who might replace Seán Ó Neachtain and still not happy. I wonder if this is just a way of Fianna Fáil garnering sympathy, but maybe not. On to the Kilfenora Céilí band which is huge fun – such skill and enthusiasm and what a huge crowd has turned up at Rathmichael School, just outside Sligo. I have a picture taken with them and enjoyed the music very much. I don't risk dancing; the dancers are far too good for me and

exceptionally fit. I meet my friend, Charlie Kelly, who introduces me to quite a few people who are vintage car enthusiasts. In the evening we go to a fundraiser for the hospital with the cyclists, only it turns out not to be a fundraiser but a drink to celebrate the day. Still we enjoy the chat. I am mystified to see the TG4 piece, all very positive stuff on the rail corridor with nothing from me. It feels like flimflam.

Tea tally: 4

Monday 11 May

We go to the Mercy Convent in Sligo for the launch of the European bus, which is late and not very well organised – but then it's their first day on the road. I don't envy them their task. Trying to explain Europe to people feels like a mountain to climb. The geography of Europe is easy but the politics of the Union are a whole different ball game. A journalist from *Le Monde* is there so I do a short interview, which makes me feel European for a moment. The elections are going on across all Europe but people only have an interest in their own country. This emphasises how out of touch we really are with the European project. We know nothing of other countries' candidates or issues or what they think of Europe or what they want out of the process. Each nation, despite its membership and despite what is being voted for, is in fact only interested in its own back yard. I do an impromptu speech to the students about the value of Europe and think how difficult it is for them to grasp it, how big the barrier is, even though most of them have probably been in Europe – Spain, France, the Algarve. We have nice photos with the Mercy girls and the Euro bus and it's time to rush to the next place.

The biggest news of the day is that Fianna Fáil finally announces that Pat the Cope Gallagher will give up his Dáil seat to stand as an MEP. This is the man who previously gave up his MEP seat to stand for the Dáil: some kind of Fianna Fáil yo-yo game. Paschal is quick to go on radio and say again how upset he is, that he was chosen by the party grass roots at a convention and that he feels aggrieved. The *Irish Independent* asks for my view and I tell them that it's the kind of 'last-minute chaos that has characterised Fianna Fáil's management of the country in the past twelve months' and that it highlights their lack of real commitment to Europe, which first came to light with their shoddy, disorganised and pathetic attempt to win a much-needed 'Yes' vote for the Lisbon Treaty last summer.

We arrive in Castlebar for the debate at the European Anti-Poverty Network (EAPN). It's tricky because it's the first of these debate-style events that I've had. I have tried really hard to get my head around the EAPN and have spent a long time on their website, but it hasn't really helped. There is too much jargon and the website is not designed for the beginner. I'm not going to begin to pretend that I know what this network really does because I don't. I'm sure I am aware of the consequences of their work but not of the organisation. This wouldn't matter ordinarily but it matters now. I have given thought to some of the subjects that I know are relevant but have no idea how the afternoon will go.

It's a formal setting in a hotel – the top table where the candidates sit, then the audience, which, I guess, comprises people who work in the poverty sector in Ireland. It's a long session – two hours and the audience has been divided into groups which spent the morning workshopping and coming up with questions for us. And they're hugely difficult subjects to deal with – immigration, funding and disability. How is anyone going to sit up there and say they will do anything other than the right thing, that they will be mindful of these needs if they are elected. As it happens I feel strongly about these issues and have chosen over the years to make many programmes about the most vulnerable groups.

I find the format difficult and feel that we are not getting to the heart of what they wanted to talk about. I say this and it opens up the conversation somewhat. I think a bit of me is 'being the producer', thinking we were all talking round in circles and failing to get to the heart of anything. Again I feel that a 'less is more' approach might have helped – to concentrate on one or two subjects and really explore them might have been more challenging and more revealing. I have the difficulty of not knowing what I can promise or commit to because I really do not know how, in this particular job, I can have any effect – never having done the job.

All the candidates are there except Fianna Fáil: perhaps that's because they would find it difficult to say 'the right thing' or to defend a record which has seen the gap between the lowest paid and the highest paid rise dramatically while they've been in office. Or maybe Pat the Cope and Paschal are locked in a room somewhere sorting out their differences. The candidates who are there work hard and I enjoy it by the end because they are real issues with real people in the front line. After it's over, we go outside and have our pictures taken – with the Euro bus which has caught up with us – and some schoolboys who are on their way home. Then I rush around Castlebar to get the last part of my daughter's birthday present. She will be sixteen tomorrow.

Belatedly, I post a card of support to Suzanne Breen, the journalist who is under pressure to reveal her sources to the PSNI for her story relating to the murder of two British soldiers at Massereene in March and the murder of Denis Donaldson three years ago. Bringing people to justice is important but it is the job of the police, not journalists. I understand the pressure she is under and to be asked to reveal sources in the public glare means having to make a decision, stand by a decision and continue to explain that decision, which is very stressful. I have no doubt that Suzanne will stand by her journalistic principles, although the risk for her – personally and professionally – is high. I admire her courage and her strength.

Tea tally: 8

Tuesday 12 May

We celebrate Roberta's sixteenth birthday with presents first thing and I find it hard to believe that my eldest is sixteen. Where have the years gone! I reflect on it as I shovel breakfast into everyone after the presents. Roberta's pleased with her gifts but she knows she's sharing her day with a distracted mother. I've been keeping an eye on the pending nurses' strike at Sligo General and I do a quick interview with Ocean FM. Then it's time for the first national debate – the *Pat Kenny Show* is in Sligo, to host the first European candidates' debate in the Glass House Hotel. It's in front of an audience.

Strangely, although I have been on many RTÉ radio programmes, including *Today with Pat Kenny*, and I have produced the programme too, today I am very anxious indeed – far more anxious than I thought I would be. I try to calculate what is causing the anxiety and the only thing that makes sense is that I am now representing a party; it's not just me. I know too that it's the first debate with Declan Ganley and he has been getting a lot of attention.

We arrive and are directed to our seats. I am right on the edge, right next to Ganley. There is hardly room to breathe as the tables are small and there is little room to place notes. We understand that the first hour will be ours and then the audience will join in. It's fairly clear that everyone has supporters in the audience and one imagines the texters are standing by, as Sean in Tubbercurry or Mary in Donegal, when in fact they are card-carrying party members who can enjoy the cloak of anonymity that texting to live shows provides.

I am thrown completely by not being mentioned in the opening remarks and it serves as a reminder of how much an outsider I am. It doesn't matter that the Labour Party has an MEP, has a share of the electorate and is the oldest party in the state – in this constituency the party is weak. Libertas and Declan Ganley are mentioned, which given that the party has no representation anywhere seems odd – mention everyone or no one. This contributes to the battle we have on our hands. We each have a chance to state our case and I get through that and begin to relax a bit. When I get a chance I raise the query about the Libertas website: when you click on the Irish website to donate, it brings you straight through to the UK website where you can donate in pounds and that it is hard to know how the party can be funded by small local donations when you can't donate in euro. I have had several people try to donate so I know it's true. Even though Ganley denies it, it's without much enthusiasm and after the break he insists you can donate in euro. The audience ask questions, specifically the Sligo cancer services campaign, Libertas and the Labour Party. There's a bit of a dispute with one of the independent candidates, Fiachra Ó Luain, which raises the thorny issue of time on the show: how long each candidate gets and on what basis a judgement about this is made.

I am relieved when it's over and I have survived. The others will be easier now once the first is done. Lunch in Osta in Sligo, which I find I can't eat as I am still too wound up. Then I settle down in the flat where Pat is now staying, having managed successfully to open an office in town, which has made all our lives easier. The *Irish Daily Mail* has asked me to write a piece about Monageer: the tragic deaths of the Dunne family, Adrian and Ciara and their children Leanne and Shania, in 2007. The report of the enquiry has just been published. In an odd way it has great resonance with the message I am trying to build about the importance of communities and that this is where we are at our best. I finish the piece and am home for birthday tea and cake. It's just so good to be there, to mark what is another special moment – sweet sixteen. Then off to the Radisson Hotel for a meeting about drugs strategy. It's one of the funniest moments of the campaign. We walk round and round and can't find the meeting anywhere. In the end I go on the web and find that the meeting was held on 12 May 2008! It was an idea of mine to make sure that whenever government ministers are in the constituency, it's important to turn up. This one was hosted by the Minister of State, Pat Carey. Now he's Chief Whip. Somehow or other, an over-zealous researcher had failed to notice the date! It's too late to be cross: just take it on the chin and breathe.

Mags and I do some organisational work instead, to get ourselves sorted out for the next few days. I try to work out which areas I need to gather information on and which issues are pressing for the campaign. I get home to say goodnight to birthday girl Roberta and wonder how she could be taller than me now, when only moments ago she was in my arms.

When I get home the family reveals that they've taken to playing the 'Shriek' game in the car; every time they see one of my posters, one or all of them shrieks. Paul says that he keeps thinking he's forgotten something when he sees me staring down from a lamp post. He probably has! As for me, I've stopped shrieking at myself now.

Tea tally: 10

Wednesday 13 May

Drive to Dublin for the Labour European manifesto launch. It's called 'Putting People, Jobs and Fairness at the Heart of Europe'. A bit of a mouthful but a good thought. It's really useful to have our views out there to be examined by anybody, anywhere. I fear that the proposed reform of the financial sector will be the hardest to implement. It's another document to read – I'm beginning to accumulate a library of documents. At least this is one I can fall back on in interviews if I need to.

I'm grateful not to have to speak although I have yet to master the standing to one side while being part of the occasion. It seems that I concentrate too much on what the speakers are saying (it's a habit from being a journalist at press conferences) so I look too serious. Good turnout from hacks. Proinsias gets a bit of teasing about his age from Michael Brennan in the *Indo* and whether, if elected, he intends to stay the five years. In response he volunteers to race Michael around the block! There is some laughing and it's the right response. We are the only party to launch a manifesto, mostly culled from other documents, but it's good to have it to refer to. The Twittering continues in lighthearted mode: Accidentally have my first cup of coffee in five years today at the launch – still recovering! My little interview with *Le Monde* has made it into the paper so there's a bit of teasing about that.

We have lunch in the Dáil bar first and a meeting with all the candidates and party high-ups. In fact it will be the last time the four candidates are together in one place before the election. It's funny – we have much in common and yet each of us is fighting a completely different battle, in different ways and with different prospects. We have the Ganley moment – what to do about him and what the impact of his campaign is. Opinion is interestingly divided. Some think he is dangerous: others that he will not get elected. Then I have a bash-up – interrogation – with David about Europe. I just need someone to ask some tougher questions: 'Why Europe?'; 'What can I offer?'; 'What's the point of being an MEP?'; and 'What difference can you make?'. These are hard questions to answer when you are only imagining the job and not doing it but they are the questions you are asked by every journalist. I think they again reveal the dearth of our understanding and our attitude to European politics: somehow it remains second-class politics to want to go to Europe. Various people have suggested that it's really a waste of time.

Do some blogging and Twittering and finish late again with a burger! Life is great! The clock is ticking; there is less than a month left now and this is when the campaign really begins to accelerate – well, that's what the experts say.

Tea tally: 7

Thursday 14 May

Start with off-radar meeting in Dublin at 8am. It's important to have some time to think and to talk to someone who is not part of the campaign and who has no vested interest in me or the party but can give some good advice about the carousel of the campaign, about what works and what doesn't. And it forces me to sit in a room and concentrate on one thing and not fret about all the other things there are to think about. I need to have a chance to face up to the things I haven't been getting right, the less-than-robust answers that I give under pressure in an interview. I have begun to realise that nothing beats practice and the need to be completely at ease with what you believe in and the message you want to get out there, every time, not just once. It's time to go back to basics: I need good examples of why Europe is good, to be specific about road safety or clean air or support for the banks, rather than macro-European stuff that people find hard to relate to. Make it mean something in their lives. I believe in Europe but how do I 'tell that story'?

I am reminded that it's far more important than Europe and its politics and policies that I am 'liked'. Is that the heart of it all – just being liked? I think you have to be liked first and foremost, then show that you are capable and have ideas. But there it is: if you're not liked in the first instance, the hill is harder – if not impossible – to climb. I can see that this is probably true: we trust people when we like them. And with that, the warning never to get 'wound up' on TV or radio or in a public debate. In the comfort of a pleasant conversation this seems easy, almost preposterously easy, but I know there are people out there who are good at winding others up – both interviewers and other interviewees, particularly seasoned politicians. So it's good to be reminded of that pitfall. I know I'm luckier than some in that I have had broadcast experience but I need to be careful not to be lulled by that because when I was wearing my other hat, it was never about me. Now it is in part about me and I haven't understood that yet, not really. Intellectually, yes, but not in truth. To go from being an individual with views where only the views are kicked about to go to being an individual who herself is the football is disconcerting. I have taken care over the years to avoid it being about me and I have never wanted it to be any other way.

Of course we talk about Declan Ganley: about how he runs his campaign, the fact that he is everywhere and getting airtime, about how he *is* the story and whether it's better to engage with him or ignore him completely. I think there is no right answer, really, that sometimes he should be ignored and sometimes challenged.

I needed that. I'd lost my way somewhere but I feel more in control as I leave, more relaxed too. I pick the others up and it's off in the rain to Athlone and a quick-fire six-minute set of questions on I 102-105 with Abie P-Bowman, Jonathan's younger brother I think it's a good format even though I don't know how well I get through it and I'll never hear it go out. Abie asks who my European political hero is. It's not the easiest question in the world and I wonder if there are any – on the grounds that in the world there is a mere handful of what we understand to be political heroes. I know that it's a sort of trick question, the kind that journalists put in to encourage the 'fatal pause' or stumble and, if you're lucky (as the journalist), the complete breakdown. Anyway I don't default to the complete obvious, which would be Proinsias de Rossa; I don't think even Proinsias would be insulted! I opt instead for

Paul Nyrup Rasumssen, President of the Party of the European Socialists. I choose him because the party has been fighting the social democrat fight in Europe and he is a man of passion who is a good role model for true social democracy. Oddly enough I feel that the words 'social democracy' don't readily translate the message: they are too opaque, difficult and academic and don't speak to people about what is at the core of this belief: a world of equality and freedom. I've earned my cup of tea and a scone!

Then on to Tuam where we stop to canvass with our local candidate, Colm Keaveney, and have a late lunch. It's a bit damp in Tuam but Colm works hard and knows a lot of people in the town. We meet the Gilmore entourage in the car park and do more canvassing, then on to Eyre Square and the Meyrick Hotel in Galway. It rains all day and the countryside looks gloomy. So much for early summer. It's time for the red dress again. We wait to go down as the room hasn't filled up and have a quiet moment in which Eamon and I gaze out on Eyre Square where there are lots of posters of him and me staring back in at us and he talks about Galway, his home county, and how he never had the chance to run in Galway and how Irish people need to feel they know their politicians. As if to prove the point, when we are going down to the function he meets some of his Dublin constituents outside the lift who are in Galway on holiday but stop to say hello and shake hands, because they know him.

The speeches go well – I feel at home in Galway and in part it's down to the warmth for Eamon in his home county. The room is warm and it's my second outing in the red dress so I feel a bit more comfortable this time. Michael D says nice things about me and I feel strange when he says again that the party is honoured to have me. I only hope that I can live up to the billing. I am happy with my own speech; I seem to strike the right note, which is always the tricky challenge. Every speech is different, every room and group has a different feel to it. I think it's a great thing to see that Eamon and Michael D – who have so much to lose if they get it wrong – still opt for speeches without autocue or notes, more from the heart.

I enjoy talking to people afterwards, shaking hands, listening to their stories. I meet Maca Hourihane. We went to school together and haven't seen each other for twenty-five years and she's been canvassing for me already, which is great. I feel the word 'change' is beginning to have traction. I meet a Roscommon man in Tuam today who says he has voted Fianna Fáil for forty years but not any more that he is fed up and feels let down. He is a quiet man, not the kind who complains easily, so I feel he really means what he says and that it doesn't come easy to him to turn his back on his lifelong loyalty. After the speeches I meet a Labour Party member, a man who says he is forty years in the party and that he has never seen anything like it, that there is a mood for change and that there was never a better time to be in Labour.

It's a good evening, the easier side of canvassing, because most people in the room are Labour or interested but I begin to realise that you have to keep in touch with the party members as much if not more than trying to talk to complete strangers. I know I didn't understand that at first. I thought that if you were signed up to Labour you didn't need to be canvassed or persuaded but actually that's completely wrong. The members are the party grass roots, they are on the ground where you can never be – in their families, at work, at play – and if they like their candidates or are impressed by them, they will say that and become your persuaders. On top of which, if they have bothered to become members and turn out to meetings, it's absolutely right and proper that they be first on the list, respected and valued and listened to. And I am trying hard to do that: listen to people in the party and learn, while trying not to make myself too much in anyone else's likeness.

It's been a long day so throwing off my heels feels good. The dress is one thing but the heels are still a bit of a struggle! I share a cup of tea with my old college friend Liz who has come to live just outside Galway. We went to UCC together light years ago and she got in touch again when she saw that I was running. It's good to see her: it's been a long time and it's good to talk to someone beyond the political circle, which becomes all-encompassing and tightens your vision.

Tea tally: 5

Friday 15 May
We're off early to the conference of the Institute of Chartered Accountants, at which Eamon is guest speaker, along with economist David McWilliams. Of course the subject is what to do with the economy. Both make good solid speeches: David certainly is a performer. Afterwards RTÉ turns up because there is an opinion poll in today's *Irish Times* which shows the Labour Party doing well and Eamon holding his position as the most popular leader. He fields a lot of questions and I stand with him, again wondering how not to look too serious.

Then it's canvass time on Shop Street. I really find this hard. There are so many of us and the public find the photographers annoying sometimes and it's not helped by the bad weather. But I think this is me: not adjusting to the scale of it and the need for speed. Given that Eamon is so popular, everyone knows him and is happy just to shake his hand. They're not quite sure what to do with me, nor I with them. I haven't mastered the art of keeping it moving but to have Eamon canvass with me is a huge bonus.

We cut loose in the early afternoon and head for Sligo. I want to be there when Professor John Crown addresses the Sligo cancer services campaign. He is a consultant medical oncologist at St Vincent's Hospital in Dublin and is internationally recognised for his progressive research into improving the effects of chemo-therapy dosage on cancer patients The meeting's in the Radisson and we get there with time for a cuppa. There is quite a good crowd and Crown speaks from the heart and for quite a while. He is interesting and engaging and believes that the fight now has to be for a centre of excellence, a ninth such centre, for the North-West region, rather than necessarily Sligo, and that there is a population in Sligo, Donegal, Leitrim and Longford to support one. 'North-West cancer care is the fight you need to fight,' is his parting shot. There are some good contributions from the floor and I think people feel inspired by Crown's enthusiasm and grateful to him for coming and for adding professional rigour to the protest. He has been an outspoken critic of the HSE and there is a feeling that they see him as critic first, then ignore whatever he says, wherever he says it.

I get to see my family and sleep in my own bed, which seems bizarre, almost like stopping off in my own life. I'm not sure I relax, though. It's difficult because the two lives are so completely different but the family knows that there is an end point to this, that this mad whirl won't go on for ever.

Tea tally: 7

Saturday 16 May

It's the worst day weather-wise. We are dogged and delayed by horrendous rain in Tuam and Galway and I find I take my mood from this weather, which doesn't help. It's hard to canvass at weekends. People have their lives and kids and are loathe to share that with politicians. We were meant to canvass again in Tuam but it's too wet so we arrive in the centre of Galway and Sabina and Michael are there as ever and we canvass for about forty minutes but we are rained off and take refuge with hot chocolate in a pub with an open fire, the King's Head. Unimaginable in May: people are wearing big coats and hats. But there is a warm response with quite a few people coming out of their way to shake hands.

I do feel we have to go elsewhere in the city, that it's too easy to do just the main street, although Fintan, one of the younger guys, says everyone recognises that this is the campaigning street in Galway and it's expected that people canvass here for everything and anything. Largely down to Michael D over the years, I imagine.

We end up taking refuge in Michael's house – literally – and I close my eyes under a rug as the rain lashes the house. I fall asleep for a while and when I wake, we make the decision that it's pointless to canvass at churches, as planned, so we leave Galway but not before Sabina insists that I take the rug with me to have in the car, along with a woolly hat – the Higgins campaign kit. Never ignore advice from the experienced!

We head for Ennis. There are lots of Paschal posters on the poles – perhaps that's their way of sending him down here. It's not raining in Ennis so we have a walk round and a short canvass. I had forgotten how much I liked Ennis; there is a great atmosphere and lots of people are out and about. I forget that normal life means going out on a Saturday night.

Today was the day the first opinion polls came out for the Europeans and I am at 6 per cent. Against Pat the Cope at 19 per cent, Jim Higgins at 20 per cent and Marian Harkin at 18 per cent, this puts me well down. Declan Ganley polls at 9 per cent but he's on Ocean dismissing it: '*The Irish Times* would say that, wouldn't they?' and he says he has 'his own research' which shows something quite different. I am not at all downhearted, which is good. I did go in with my eyes open and I know that Labour can't suddenly come to the North-West and paint it red. Eamon rings to reassure me, which I appreciate, and says that we will be concentrating very hard now on Galway, Clare and Westmeath, which is where we are strong. Marian Harkin said on radio that she is hardly known in Westmeath or Longford but that figures, as her core vote is in Sligo and Leitrim. SF is on 10 per cent which is good for them so we have to try to take some of that away too.

It's funny to be the subject of an opinion poll, to be on a list somewhere and be part of that process even if all these polls have to be taken with a pinch of salt. Nessa Childers looks good in Leinster at 17 per cent and Alan Kelly is on 12 per cent, which is probably a bit disappointing for him: his will be a tight fight for the third seat. T mails me and says she's enjoyed the pictures in the paper but that I look 'fragile as paper' and 'must eat'. I have lost half a stone so far so I guess I should be careful but when you're running from pillar to post it's difficult to eat and to feel well. It's an unnatural existence after all. Just three weeks left.

Tea tally: 5 (and one cup of hot chocolate!)

Sunday 17 May

Ennis for Masses at nine, ten and eleven. It's cold and windy but we manage the nine o'clock Mass and have breakfast before the ten. It's unseasonable weather, cold and windy, which means people are rushing through and not keen to stop. We run into the church afterwards to retrieve abandoned leaflets and find only four and are heartened. People are happy to take them so maybe they will even read them.

We follow on with a canvass with our town council candidate, Paul O'Shea, and get a very good response here. People are very chatty and engaged and ask lots of questions. It's funny when you think you're standing outside Dunnes with people's trolleys and bits and pieces, talking about the Lisbon Treaty and why, when I live in Sligo, I think I can represent people in Clare. There was quite high recognition for me and that's always encouraging but you have to remember all the people who don't stop and who are never going to vote for you.

We have a quick sandwich and aim for the Siege of Ennis, which is the world record event to have as many people doing the 'Siege of Ennis' dance in one place at one time as is humanly possible. And what happens? The heavens open and the rains of the last year seem to fall upon all of us. Mags lends me her coat which, along with the Labour umbrella, diminishes the impact a bit. Irish people are resilient and there are plenty of umbrellas but it's hard to dance and to canvass in those conditions. I did have a go, though! Declan Ganley and Libertas are there with lots of leaflets. People are warm and encouraging – probably because they admire our effort, but in the end the rain simply becomes too much for us and we have to abandon ship. We get back to the car and quite literally I put on my pyjamas because I am soaked. Am I glad of Sabina's rug! I feel sorry for the organisers; it was such a great idea. There was plenty of space and it seemed well organised but they could do nothing about the rain.

And we are now driving like mad people to Donegal town for a fundraiser with Michael D! It's at moments like these that the size of the constituency morphs into the size of the challenge. Of course we have tea – at least today the excuse is the wet. I find myself trapped in the pyjamas and can't get out of the car when we stop at a garage! European candidate in pyjama moment isn't quite the image I was seeking.

We pile into the hotel in Donegal and change into posh clothes. The fundraiser has been organised locally by my friend K and is hugely enjoyable. Michael D is, as ever, delightful and generous. I make a speech and am proud to introduce Michael D, who is popular wherever he goes. The Donegal Tenors entertain and it's nice to be able to enjoy them. They add the right touch to the evening. I do an interview with *Donegal Democrat* journalist, Paddy Meehan, and we end up talking about the cancer services in Sligo. There and then I am struck by an idea: I say I am going to challenge Mary Harney to travel on a bus from Donegal to Galway – in fact from Glencolmcille to Galway – as a patient recently had to do. It seems like a good idea to raise the profile of the campaign and to make it personal to Mary Harney. That's one of the lessons we learned at *World in Action*: people respond better to stories when you place the responsibility at someone's door – not just the door of government, which is invisible and impersonal. In this story, it is women who are largely affected because of breast cancer and Mary Harney is the Minister for

Health who has presided over the proposed move from Sligo. She will never have to sit on a bus so is always going to be out of touch with reality. I'm happy to throw down the gauntlet, which means I will have to organise the bus. Now it's definitely time for a glass of wine and to forget the damp Ennis afternoon. We have raised some money and, believe it or not, now drive back to Sligo – to be in the right place for the Ocean FM debate tomorrow morning.

Tea tally: 8

Monday 18 May
The worst day for quite a while. The weather is poor and I am tired after yesterday and desperate for a bit of heat and light. We arrive at Ocean on time. We're all there and I'm sharing a mike with Pat the Cope. Declan Ganley has a mike of his own. The politics of mike distribution have become quite important but the show's producer or presenter has the last word and can always pull up the fader and cut you off.

Paschal Mooney talks again of his unhappiness about having had Pat the Cope added to the ticket when Sean Ó Neachtain quit. I am surprised that this unhappiness is still his first card to play and find it tedious now but perhaps Paschal is working the sympathy vote. The debate goes well enough and presenter Niall Delaney keeps us all on track most of the time. It's long, though, and I wonder what people really think of it. Will what we say make a difference? I guess it could if you screwed up really badly or insulted someone or walked off in high dudgeon but I suspect it can't be as much of an opinion-maker as we think it is when we are locked in studio. There is a bit of a shouting match at one stage but I'm not sure people notice when you *don't* shout. By that I mean that

I don't know if the audience cares that some people stay quiet and the others get into a fight. I don't blame them if they don't.

What can come across then is that politicians apparently don't care about the audience and are prepared to bicker amongst themselves. In reality I think that everyone is getting tired. The hours and the travel are beginning to tell, the pressure is on and it shows in a small room where suddenly the risks are illuminated. The studio does feel very small and claustrophobic. It's also because the issues are so difficult to address coherently and in a way that the electorate can understand because MEPs don't rush off to Europe with a list of demands, formed from a list of promises, then come back with all of them to deliver to a grateful audience. It's so hard to quantify in what way an MEP is successful or not.

But the pressure is rising. It's rising for Fianna Fáil everywhere across the country and especially for Paschal, who remains unhappy. It's on Declan Ganley because he knows Libertas has no future unless he is elected. It's on Marian Harkin to hold her seat against Ganley and it's on Sinn Féin to perform well. Mary Lou McDonald is under great pressure in Dublin as they don't want to be in a position where they have no MEPs. I suspect that Joe O'Reilly of Fine Gael feels under pressure and would like to believe there is a second Fine Gael seat. I'm not convinced of this as Pat the Cope has very strong support in Donegal. Of course I'm under pressure too, to do well and to run a good campaign and to fly the flag for Labour but I know that I don't share the pressure to get the seat. Not that we ever say that out loud: indeed it's banned from conversation. We are here to win, we fight to win, we want a seat: it's important to keep that mantra going because it provides motivation and self-belief.

Deputy party leader Joan Burton has arrived in Sligo to canvass with me, which is great. She comes out to Ocean to do a detailed interview about the economy and I sit in and listen (and learn) and am grateful not to have to do more radio today. We head for the Showgrounds, home of the Bit o' Red, the Sligo Rovers, where we had planned to do some filming with the girls from Ursuline College, to highlight the training they get from Sligo Rovers as a perfect example of community and its strength. My middle daughter, Grace, has gathered some of her friends who've been enjoying the training; that's what gave me the idea. There has been some confusion about permissions and we are asked to leave, although not before we have kicked the ball around a bit and been filmed by RTÉ. I am upset because I didn't want to cause any problems for the club or for RTÉ. The kids are a bit disappointed too. RTÉ agrees to pick up with us in Boyle tomorrow.

We drive to Boyle for lunch with Joan and out town councillor, Willy Tiernan. Our local council candidate, John Feely, joins us from Carrick-on-Shannon. My daughter, Roberta, comes too, to see what canvassing is like close-up. She is in Transition Year, so it's a good opportunity. We have a meeting with the town council which I hadn't anticipated: I probably wasn't paying attention when I was briefed. They make a presentation to us and we have to respond there and then. I wouldn't normally turn up to a meeting without knowing what the subject of discussion is but this is politics and I have to think on my feet. I take my cue from Joan, who doesn't hesitate, so I pick a couple of things to respond to, especially the battle for heritage status for the town. I advise them to get in touch with Clones, which is having a similar battle, and perhaps to share ideas with them as to how to proceed.

I feel as if I managed to be coherent enough but there is a big lesson here: make sure I am completely briefed for every visit – no surprises. It's a discourtesy to turn up and breeze through. We canvass through the town and arrive at Drumderrig Nursing Home. I really enjoy meeting the people who live there. They remind me that the vulnerable are there and often invisible as we race round and how easy it is to ignore their voice because they do not shout. There is a gentleness here that is missing in most other environments.

We meet Mary, who is a hundred and four. I wonder what she thinks of politics now and, as we talk, I try to imagine what she has seen in more than a century of life in Ireland. She really has cause to base her politics on the civil war as she lived through it – unlike others who were born after it but hold fast to its significance as if they were witnesses. I find the reluctance to move on from what our fathers believed in really difficult to understand. The fervour was right for them then – politics was alive and a matter of life and death in a way that has never been repeated in Ireland – but the iron grip it still has on political thinking surprises me. Why is it the frame around which everything is built? Enough philosophy. The hospital has its own staffing problems and a unit lies idle because of that.

Back to Sligo. Joan meets party members. We drink tea. I go to the office to do an interview with Today FM – always difficult down the line. I am cold and feeling unwell but guess it's just a bit of overload. And it's still raining!

Tea tally: 6

Tuesday 19 May

Time to canvass on telly – with RTÉ in Boyle, The sun makes a rare appearance so I do my interview with North-West correspondent Eileen Magnier about why I'm standing. That's all fine till we start the canvass in the local bakers with our candidate, Peadar Markey. I'm confident he has taken me in to a place where he is known; indeed somewhere in the recesses of my brain I decide that the person I am about to shake hands with is Peadar's sister. Imagine my surprise when, after I have smiled and introduced myself, the woman says she is anti-Europe and is not sure whether she will vote at all. Get out of that one! I do my best, breaking all the rules of canvassing by spending valuable time trying to persuade her, and by the end she says that maybe she will vote but I'm not so sure and don't think it will be for me. Of course I know that only a fragment of this stuff ever gets used on TV and maybe people think that those events are staged to make the candidate look capable even when people disagree. Well this certainly was no set-up. We go in and out of shops and talk to people on the street and it's all fine after that. After we say goodbye to RTÉ, we're on the road to Galway. Again.

On the way I write an article for the *Mail* about Frank Dunlop, the Fianna Fáil bagman who has just been sentenced to two years' imprisonment and a fine of €30,000, the longest sentence ever handed out for corruption in Ireland. He arrived to court in a silver top-of-the-range Mercedes and left in a prison van. Judge Frank O'Donnell said he believed Mr Dunlop had actively undermined the confidence of the public in democracy. That's polite. How the world turns topsy. I remember when Frank was a well groomed, successful man who had the world at his feet and who could tell a mere nobody like me – otherwise known as a nosy and annoying journalist – to buzz off. Frank was always far too polite to say that but that was what he meant. He did the usual PR stuff of telling me things I didn't want to know or refusing to cooperate, although he was always charming. Now I find myself driving in a car with my face all over it, writing about the downfall of Dunlop. I had more than my suspicions at the time but the fact that it has come to this is staggering. It's very depressing too that this was going on, that it was part of the system of government, that a man like Frank Dunlop, seen as a pillar of the political community, should in truth be running round with bags of cash and handing them over to people in bars and hospitals, to buy influence and ultimately to make money and line his own pockets and those of others. I finish the piece in the back of the car, which is difficult as my laptop screen is always too dark.

Time to put on the face, the smile and the make-up and get out of the car again. This time we're with a great big gang of people canvassing for Derek Nolan, the Labour candidate in the east ward of Galway City Council. There are so many people out canvassing that we have to divide ourselves up. What a luxury. There is quite a different knack to this way of canvassing: people knock for you and you stand and wait for a door to open, then appear. I like meeting people on their doorsteps better than in shops, where I always feel awkward. It's a beautiful evening in Galway and the people with me are experienced and very enthusiastic, which makes it much easier. We get a positive response although there are quite a few empty houses, not surprising because the sun is shining and that's quite a rare sight these days.

We have a funny moment when we knock on one door and a

gang of students answers and recognises the person canvassing with me as one of their college tutors. It's exam time but they certainly don't have the air of studious students! Another woman is determined that she will not be voting for anybody but when I start talking about Michael D, she smiles and says he is different and a decent man so I introduce her to Michael D's son, Michael, who is with me on the doorstep! She sees the funny side of that. On the way back, I draft a statement for release tomorrow, supporting journalist Suzanne Breen:

O'Keeffe Supports Right of Suzanne Breen to Maintain Confidentiality of Source

> I would like to add my voice in support of *Sunday Tribune* Northern Editor Suzanne Breen in her defence of her right to protect her source. As somebody who has been in a similar position, I have no doubt that Ms Breen is right to maintain the confidentiality of the source she quoted in her story about the Real IRA.
>
> The heavy-handed reaction to her piece represents a disturbing infringement of press freedom. As a journalist in a free and open society, Suzanne Breen is entitled, indeed obliged, to unearth the truth, however unpalatable that truth may be. While the use of accountable quotes from attributed sources is certainly the preferred option when writing a news story, from time to time, such as in this case, public interest is best served by the publication of information that is gathered from anonymous sources.

It is a cornerstone of journalism that sources be protected, and I welcome the commitment by the *Sunday Tribune* to vigorously defend Suzanne Breen's right to keep her sources confidential.

Tea tally: 7

Wednesday 20 May

I don't think there was much time for tea today. It was such a busy day but very productive – a targeted canvass in a way, organised by candidate Niall McNelis. I started with the dole queue in Galway, as I wanted to talk to people directly about their experience. It's easy to talk about unemployment in that abstract way and it's much better to go and shake hands and ask people to tell their story. Needless to say there was a long queue. Lots of people didn't want to talk to me and who could blame them? Those who did talk were quietly angry or distraught. For many, this was the first time they had been out of work and they were bewildered, ashamed and despairing about how they would cope. And it's not as if there is a great quick-fix solution so it's no surprise that governments retreat to ivory towers. How hard it is to look people in the eye when you have no real answers. The current government has shown it has no will to come up with anything that looks like an answer – no innovation, no leadership, no solutions of any kind, not even temporary or part solutions.

The dole queue creates another dilemma. TV3 arrives to film me on the canvass. I take responsibility because when they asked me for my schedule the previous day I gave it to them. I should have edited it out but I forgot to connect the television with the dole queue. So now I have to put my foot down and insist they film very carefully so no one is identifiable. I wear my television producer's hat and know all the tricks but I can see that people in the queue are not happy. I'm not either – so lesson learned.

As it turns out a long email exchange ensues with one woman who says that we behaved badly and that she was filmed. She complains to the local radio, Galway Bay FM, who have the decency to call me and ask for my side of the story. I explain to her and to Galway Bay that this is not the case, that I have been given assurances by TV3 that no faces will appear and that I am satisfied that TV3 understands the situation. Her face does not appear. I can't help noticing the irony: I have spent my professional life ensuring that the faces of the vulnerable do not appear in any of the programmes I have produced and now here I am trying to ensure it again – but without the final say-so.

We go up the street to the hub of the Galway stopover for the round-the-globe Volvo Ocean Race and meet the people behind the scenes, who are in the final throes of preparation. I hadn't quite realised the enormity of their task until then: it really is staggering. Marketing manager Gwen O'Sullivan walks us through the village-to-be and there is a frenzy of hammering and banging as they build the stage for the free open-air concerts. There is a buzz and excitement, in marked contrast to the dole queue. Enda O'Coineen, who is one of the main movers and shakers behind this event, joins us and explains that getting Fáilte Ireland involved was major, as it isn't that organisation's normal terrain. They now have a very important partnership and he hopes it will serve as a blueprint for how things could be done in the future. O'Coineen and John Killeen of bitumen producers, Cold

Chon, have organised themselves as 'Let's Do It Galway', a simple but attractive name which seems to reflect their enthusiasm for making the city better.

Time for tea and a meeting with the people who run COPE, the homeless charity in Galway. Michael Brennan from the *Irish Independent* joins us and we have a robust conversation about the level of homelessness, the work that needs to be done and the constant funding question. Then to a meeting with the Chamber of Commerce, which is really informative and useful: inward investment, infrastructure, the perennial Galway traffic crisis and stronger links with Europe.

Michael interviews me between stops so it's pretty hectic. He asks an interesting question – about immigrants taking Irish jobs and what it means and what the solution is. This is one of the 'elephant in the room' moments. Immigration isn't mentioned a lot but when it is, the context is often negative and the 'taking our jobs' argument is the one proffered most. It's hard to defend this one: I mean in the sense that those who want to build barriers and keep people out are by their very nature quite vehement and unmovable so it's hard to find a way through their opposition. I explain to Michael that I believe people are angry and complain about immigrants when in truth they are angry about their own position and with our own government. They need a soft target, someone who is weaker than themselves, because it restores some sense of power to them when they feel powerless and there is always the hope that if people are unwelcoming, the immigrants might actually leave. Any action seems better than none when you are feeling helpless and largely abandoned by government. I suspect Michael is sorry he asked!

I think we manage lunch and I do an interview with Ocean about the nurses' strike which is due to start tomorrow, then have an interesting conversation with Simon Comer about the need for cycle lanes in Galway which I can see will be difficult because the streets are so narrow – but if ever a city was made for cycling, it was Galway. On a day like today, when finally the sun is shining and it's suddenly summer, a bicycle is a no-brainer, especially when you watch the endless queues of traffic snake their way round the tiny streets. Certainly our cities need to do more to encourage cycling and perhaps the bicycle hire scheme which is due to come to Dublin soon would also work in Galway. We desperately need to take the emphasis off cars.

Then a very interesting meeting with the brains behind GLUAS, Professor Lewis Lesley. I think it's a wonderful idea – a kind of light rail for Galway and other places. The estimated cost is €200 million and it would provide an electricity powered tram-like system through the centre of Galway with an engineering system that minimises construction cost and the associated disruption. Whatever happens, there has to be some solution to the traffic in Galway – it really is ruining the most beautiful part of the city and causing untold stress to those who live and work there. I am really taken with this and would love to know precisely why it has met with so much opposition. Yes, it is a risk but all new systems are a risk, as Alexander Graham Bell found out when he tried to sell the patent for his new telephone to the president of Western Union for $100,000. The company dismissed it as a 'toy', two years later tried to buy the patent for $25 million. Bell and his original partners refused to sell, becoming millionaires themselves, as the 'toy' became the must have of the late 19th century. I enjoy talking to people who want to change the way things are done or have a new take on an old problem. There isn't enough of that – imagination, innovation. Great bodies do indeed move slowly.

It's been a busy but fruitful day, learning about Galway, about what makes the city tick, about who is doing business there and how great it is in the warm weather. It feels like a different country and a different exercise, campaigning in the sunshine. I also have some very useful conversations with farming experts and economists about agribusiness and agriculture, mindful that the IFA debate is tomorrow. Farmers are one community that is really struggling but is used to speaking out so I am expecting a long and vocal session.

I start writing my piece for the *Mail* for Saturday – about the Ryan report. It's almost too much to comprehend, despite the fact that I was there in the beginning and was the first to push the truth about child abuse and the Catholic Church. The report is shocking in its baldness, in its truth. Until now, much of this was dismissed as hearsay, exaggeration – call it what you will – but the official reporting changes its status and gives it a presence and makes it real, which is all the victims could ever hope for. Their testimony can no longer be pushed into dark corners. The revelation that this government made a deal with the Church in the dying days of their last term is sickening. It boils down to a pay-off really; give us €128 million now and we'll make sure you don't have to pay any more later, no matter what happens!

Mags is threatening to take my laptop away as I am supposed to go to bed but spend another two hours working – as I do most nights. The learning curve is steep.

Tea tally: 6

Thursday 21 May

Today's headlines tell the tragic stories behind yesterday's publication of the long-awaited Ryan Report. A nation's horror is exposed in detail and with the official backing of the commission's investigation into child abuse at state-run and church-run industrial schools. It seems to me that the government is hoping it will slide away into oblivion, part of our past that should stay in the past. The fact that it is a catalogue of horror will help victims to some extent, because their evidence and their stories are written down for the first time, but it seems to me not to be enough, to be only the beginning and long overdue. I don't feel from the way the government has responded that it is really connected to what has happened, to what it means to the moral fibre of our country that this went on for such a long time and that so many citizens colluded in it, through negligence, carelessness, selfishness, badness and ultimately through a wholesale dismissal of the voiceless poorest of the poor.

I find a lovely photo of me canvassing in Galway in the middle of the *Examiner*; never did something seem so out of place in the face of something like the Ryan Report.

Today is the all-out nurses' strike in Sligo. I have been vigorous on radio and in print in encouraging talks to continue and outraged at the prospect that frontline nurses will be the ones to lose their jobs. Again it is the vulnerable who will be affected – the sick in this case. I can't imagine that Sligo Hospital was awash with nurses and that throwing a few overboard won't be noticed. Indeed the figures suggest that the staffing levels are quite tight already. I know the nurses didn't want to go on strike: nurses never do. Our team in Sligo, Kirsten Gordon and Pat Cooper, take my support to the picket line; I've tried to work a way of getting to Sligo but it just won't fit in with my other commitments.

It's a very busy day as there are two debates this evening – Trócaire and the IFA – with a kind of overlap going on. We have explained to Trócaire that we will have to leave early and they understand. I spend some of my morning finalising my preparations for Trócaire – again this is a tricky debate because the area is vast and complicated and it is difficult to know where the MEP's job touches it directly, except in the obvious way of being a public representative and continuing to keep overseas aid and development on the agenda. Trócaire's priorities are simple and include ensuring that the EU will give 'more and better aid' and will pledge to end 'global hunger'. This at a time when the aid budget in Ireland is itself under threat. I have enormous admiration for those who continue the work for communities that remain impoverished because of the inequalities in our system but I know I will feel a bit out of my depth here as knowledge of this area is not my strongest suit.

We canvass in the morning on Shop Street. I take my poster with me and introduce it to people. It makes them smile, which can't be bad, and the weather remains good. There is much excitement about the imminent arrival of the Volvo race and the city is putting its best foot forward with paint and flowers and general cleaning up.

Then we head for the hotel for the Trócaire debate. The independent candidate, Michael McNamara, and myself are the only ones there. It goes fine but I know I am depending too much on commonsense rather than on first-hand knowledge. I start by proffering a red card to Libertas for introducing the idea of a 'blue card' for EU citizens to work in the EU – it's a racist trick on their part. They dress it up as 'security' but, in reality, it's another way of building a wall to keep 'certain people' out. Of course the red card includes my website and says 'Vote 1 for Europe' on it – never miss an opportunity to canvass! Then into the van and drive like mad people to the McWilliam Park Hotel in Claremorris for the IFA debate. Now this really is a test of strength, to drop one topic and move to the next. Fortunately for me, farming is one area I do know so it's not so difficult.

The big room is very full. IFA president, Padraig Walshe, opens the debate. The discussion goes on a long time. We each have to state our case at the start so I explain that I am a dairy and food scientist and that I started my career specialising in agricultural, then agribusiness journalism and that I investigated the beef industry, resulting in the Beef Tribunal. The audience is feisty and vocal and gets completely furious with Pat the Cope, who actually says he is 'not part of the government' when there is an argument about the cancelling of certain sheep payments. In general they are not a happy bunch and with prices collapsing all round, it's not difficult to see why. I get a warm reception and it seems as if exposing problems in the beef industry is something farmers welcomed. When the debate is over we are offered tea and sandwiches. I'm so hungry I would nearly eat beef at this stage and I'm happy that both those intense debates are over. I enjoy the sandwiches, then go back to the bar, drink tea and circulate for a while longer. People are warm and friendly and I guess it's because it is Fine Gael territory and I am not the enemy. Not everything can be valued in terms of votes and this is an occasion to show that the Labour Party has some strength and depth when it comes to farmers. It adds to the good work that Sean Sherlock, the party spokesperson on agriculture, has been doing.

Time for bed and we head for Mullingar – that's what right-minded people do in the middle of the night. Thank goodness new volunteer Cormac McConville has joined to help out with the endless driving On the way we talk about the value of 'I think' versus 'I believe'. Mags believes that I say 'I think' when I mean 'I believe' and having heard her argument 'I believe' she is right. I think we check in at 2.30am and I know I have an early start because I have to finish the *Mail* piece, then get out canvassing. I resist the laptop and sleep.

Tea tally: 9

Friday 22 May

I file the piece on the Ryan report for the *Mail* by 10am and am delighted to meet the deadline with so much else going on. I am more upset by Ryan than I thought I could be and the piece reflects this and my pessimism about the future:

> Every one of us has celebrated the joy of a new life. Be it sister, cousin, wife, mother or daughter, we have all sent cards, flowers or money to mark the moment of a new life. Those of us lucky to have children of our own never want to forget the moment of their birth: the newness of life, the enormous potential and the purity that their tiny frames represent.
>
> How then have we arrived in a place where our nation is torn asunder by report after report into the way our children have been treated? The stories they tell

are not simply bitter memories etched on the faces of elderly people up and down Ireland and in lost corners of England. Neither can they be viewed as the end of our dirty laundry from a different century; recent tragedies of Monageer and Roscommon show all too clearly that there are plenty of cracks for those tiny frames to fall through.

Let me tell you what this ugly story is about. When I investigated child abuse and the Catholic clergy for Granada Television's *World in Action*, it was early 1992. I travelled around the UK, the US and Ireland talking to a huge range of people about their experiences and their lives. I met Irish men in their seventies, with hollow eyes, who had run away to Birmingham and London to escape the pain. I met American women who spoke with therapy on their tongues to try to cope. And when I came to Ireland, I met a stone wall.

Oh, there were victims all right: young women, young boys, older women. They were hard to find but once they realised that someone wanted to listen they talked. And their common themes were anger and shame about the physical abuse, then a profound sadness that they had been ignored and abandoned by society, by their own people. Some of them had tried to voice their stories but deaf ears prevailed.

I did my best. I rang up and wrote to all kinds of people who would know – social workers, doctors, therapists, centres for women – but the lateral thinking exercise yielded little response. In some cases I got downright refusal but, more often than not, I got vague fudge about not knowing enough to say or not thinking it was appropriate to talk to me or not thinking it was really that common! There are several hundred ways to say 'No' but I recognise a 'No' when I see one. Not one of these respectable people in respectable jobs could find the courage to come out and speak out on behalf of fellow Irishmen and Irishwomen because they were too concerned about how they might look, about how it might affect their prospects. And they were too afraid to cast a stone in the direction of the all powerful, omnipresent Catholic Church.

The programme was made and broadcast in the summer of 1992. Its chief truths were simple: that members of the clergy had sexually abused children and that the Church had conspired in all these countries and in others – successfully – to hide the truth when potential victims or their families threatened it. Was it welcomed? Did people jump and pursue the truth? No, they wrote to newspapers and rang radio stations to complain – about me! I wasn't surprised but I *was* angry on behalf of those people who had taken courage in their hands to speak out. The face of the mother of a young abused boy in Castlerea is etched on my brain for eternity.

Consider then that a further seventeen years passed before the publication of the report of the Child Abuse Commission. It is lengthy and its findings are grave and it stabs through the heart of any right-thinking member of the human race. How pathetic then for the Tánaiste to stand in the Dáil and ask for quiet reflection and calm before a Dáil debate – the week after next! Unparliamentary language is not required, Mary – just compassion, outrage and a promise to do something, anything, anything more than you have done. And no, not a monument with Bertie Ahern's apology on it. That's not the answer. How could any public representative stand up and sound so disconnected, so apathetic?

The Tánaiste's response tilts at the deep wound in our collective psyche. Our years of neglectful behaviour, of fear, dark secrets and truths never to be told have bred a dangerous idea somewhere that it's OK to have a group of people in society who are less deserving, who belong in the shadows, who are not really part of our Ireland.

And the truth is that they *were* excluded from our Ireland. Many of the children abused – mentally, physically and sexually – across the industrial schools and by parish clergy were poor or came from families without influence or who were not connected to the so-called pillars of the community; priests, Gardaí and politicians. Indeed the report confirms this in its own findings. They could complain but no one would listen. They could ask for their children back and have the door shut in their face. It is no accident that the most vulnerable children are preyed on; paedophiles and bullies always choose the weakest ones, the ones with no support system; the voiceless.

And in not treating them equally, we took the next logical step: we locked them away where possible. We have shut people in asylums and in back rooms and not mentioned them. Children and adults with mental disabilities were routinely airbrushed from family events and, in some cases, from family mention. I have known them, seen them and met them. You have too. And since the institutions themselves felt powerful enough to ignore complaints and concerns, hiding the offending priest, brother or nun by moving them on was par for the course.

In situations in which the offending parties could not be incarcerated, our society locked away the answers. There could be no surprise then that Justice Mary Laffoy, the first head of the Commission Enquiry, resigned the post in 2003 because the Department of Education failed to comply with requests for documents. Yesterday's report confirms that thousands of files relating to abuse in the Department of Education are missing without explanation. Six years ago, under enormous pressure from the Catholic institutions, the Commission committed to keeping secret the identity of the abusers and that promise has been kept in full. And at the publication of the findings, Mr Justice Sean Ryan head of the enquiry, refused to answer any questions from journalists.

How can you prosecute nameless, faceless perpetrators? You can't! So the Church will endure a week or so of public criticism but by avoiding the courts, it avoids the real pain. More importantly it prevents victims using the due process of the law to seek redress. Oh and don't forget that the Church also managed, with a Fianna Fáil government, to negotiate favourable settlement terms in 2002: an indemnity against all future claims if they paid out an agreed sum of €128 million. Only a small part was money: the rest was property. In this country one pillar of power talking to another can always manage to do business at the expense of the voiceless. What did the victims manage to negotiate? They couldn't even get into the room when Justice Ryan was publishing the report: this is what passes for progress. This is democracy – Irish style.

And around another corner is Children's Ombudsman Emily Laffoy doing battle with the HSE and the Department of Health for access to information for her investigation into the Child Protection Audit of the Catholic Church dioceses. She is asking. They are refusing. And they know they can get away with it because they look around and see everyone else at the same thing.

A whole family dies in Monageer under the eyes of several agencies and when the report is published; lots of blank pages: 'legally sensitive' information and recommendations we could not see! Everyone knew something was not right with this family and around the country there are other families like theirs. Indeed social workers say there are 1500 children at risk of abuse or neglect in the country today, which means the figure is actually higher. One social worker told me of a family where the two young children are strapped in buggies all day, turned to the wall. We are talking of horrors behind closed doors. And are we coping better than we did fifty years ago? Social workers say these at-risk children will only receive help if they 'escalate into an emergency'. And then? Well there's no 24-hour emergency helpline available, nor one promised, so such an escalation does not guarantee help either. And you can't help a dead body.

No, this ugly story is set to continue because we are not yet ready to stand up to scrutiny and we don't understand accountability. The Commission's report compiled what we already knew but, instead of it being a turning point in our behaviour, it will serve as a fig-leaf, a pretence of progress when behind it the system continues to perpetuate secrecy and the protection of the guilty.

We canvass in Mullingar, on the main street, then at the shopping centre. It goes well and someone from the *Mail* calls to say they're happy with the piece. We do an interview with the *Westmeath Topic* and get a great photo of me with the statue of Joe Dolan which I Twitter. Then more canvassing. I am angry with Mary Harney's office because of the lack of response to the invitation to come on the bus next week. They don't want to know and don't even engage. I issue this statement:

North-West Cancer Care – Harney Misses the Bus and Misses the Point

Labour Euro candidate Susan O'Keeffe, who invited the Minister for Health Mary Harney to accompany her on a bus travelling from Glencolmcille, County Donegal, to Galway, is disappointed that Minister Harney has not given this request the urgency it requires.

Susan O'Keeffe said: 'This is the route that the Minister Harney wants cancer patients to take, when they need to travel for treatment in University College Hospital Galway. Sligo currently provides cancer services for many patients in the North-West, but under Minister Harney's plans, that facility is to close, and patients will have to travel to UCHG, from places as far away as Letterkenny and Buncrana. Given that many of these patients are reliant on public transport, that means that the journey to hospital will be by bus!

'I wrote to Minister Harney earlier this week and invited her to join me on that trip. The best her office could come up with was a reply from one of her officials to say: "The Minister for Health Mary Harney TD has asked me to thank you for your letter concerning cancer services in the North-West and to let you know that it is receiving attention." That is not good enough, Minister. You should have accepted the invitation immediately to get first-hand experience of the journey patients will have to travel. I am inviting you once again to get on

the bus with me and experience first-hand the ordeal
that others travelling for radiotherapy will be forced to
endure.'

One is never sure how statements are received but I believe it
is always worth having it on the record.

I get the van washed and grab a sandwich in the bar in the
Mullingar Park Hotel, while the hotel staff struggle with a huge
wedding. Then back out for four hours with and Labour councillor
Mick Dollard and local council candidate Gerry Sheridan on the
doorsteps. We do a hundred houses in four hours, made to look
easy by Mick because he knows every door of every house and is
thorough in reminding people about the election and explaining
how they need to vote and what to do with the ballot papers. It's
a lot to ask of people, to make sense out of all the ballot papers at
the same time, all asking different things. Mick takes no chances,
writing it down for people and explaining it clearly and easily.
It's gruelling but I enjoy it. It's Gerry's first time, too, so we have
something in common and I think we both recognise that Mick
is a hard act to follow. Am exhausted so sleep well.

Tea tally: 4

Saturday 23 May

We have less than two weeks left. It's hard to know what to do
except keep doing what we have been doing. I have a bit of a
chance to catch up on e-mails and reading material. I prepare a
new leaflet because I've found that people look at the one I have
and ask: 'But what are your policies?' I had never thought the
leaflet made a difference to people but quite clearly that's not

true. The leaflet I had said who I was and what I stood for. I have written a new one which is about my vision for this constituency. I have genuinely tried to listen and talk to people and incorporate what I have heard and learned so it's not what *I* think but what I have interpreted that people want. One thing I have thought, though, is that the North-West in particular has dined out on the *béal bocht* approach, emphasising the negative, looking at the glass half-empty, through the eyes of a Dublin and east coast that have always been given everything. That's not to say there isn't some truth in this there is but it strikes me that it's always better to look at strengths as a way forward. So I have developed the idea that this constituency, in this century, should be the engine-driver of the Irish economy, that our turn has come and that we have plenty of assets for making this happen. I've run it past a few reputable economists and others and no one has laughed it completely out of school. I spend some considerable time editing the leaflet so that I can get complex ideas into accessible language that has meaning and is, above all, optimistic. I do seek several opinions before I send it to the party but it gets the green light and off it goes to the printer. I realise that the leaflet is more important than I had understood, that if people are curious about me they will read it. There is little point in making huge effort talking to people, doing well on radio and knowing the material, then forgetting the leaflet. Lesson learned. It all matters. This is the text of the leaflet:

Two major crises are facing the world; the breakdown of the financial system and the perils of climate change. By an accident of geography the North-West has more to offer in our changing world than at any time in its past. Together we have the opportunity to drive a vision of the North-West as the new engine for the Irish economy, using our great natural strengths and our existing expertise and by building on our existing strong sense of community.

I want this vision of our constituency, as a generator of smart green growth, to underpin the work I do in Europe as an MEP.

There are five major categories to create jobs and a new strong North-West economy.

1. Green energy/green products
2. Agriculture, food, fisheries, forestry
3. Tourism
4. Media and communications
5. Biomedical engineering

To drive this vision of the North-West I will commit to be an ambassador for the region and to:

- Pursuing strong rural development which involves the farming community directly and is not driven by poorly-funded schemes
- Pursuing every avenue at home and in Europe to ensure a commitment to broadband rollout across the eleven counties
- Pursuing a decent road network for the whole region

- Pursuing commitment for the completion of the Western Rail Corridor and supporting projects like the Gluas light rail network proposal for Galway city
- Harnessing the enthusiasm, initiative and knowledge of various people and projects already in the region to strengthen joined-up thinking and communication and reduce duplication of effort

In between, we try to cross the 't's and dot the 'i's for Tuesday's bus journey. It's a big undertaking because it has to work and it must not do any damage to the Sligo cancer campaign that has been working so hard for so long. We have talked to members of the campaign about how they will support it and some of the women have agreed to travel with us. For them, that's a big sacrifice because, although they are all survivors, some still have poor health and get tired easily.

One of our supporters has asked me to raise the pay that Eircom directors receive. Eircom is in great difficulties with debt of around €3.7 billion. Many of the directors who were involved when Australian investment company Babcock & Brown bought Eircom have now resigned. All were receiving salaries in the half-million euro range. I'm not sure I can raise this one but yet again it's a case, like the bankers, of large salaries being paid to people who seem to have brought companies to their knees.

We now have a new team member: David Kitching, who has been working with the Party of European Socialists (PES) in Europe. That's good because he can take on some of the driving. He joins Kirsten Gordon, a Labour Party intern, who's been helping Pat in the Sligo office. The lean machine is still lean so we head for Athlone and canvass there in the afternoon. It's a sunny day and people are pleasant and our team is working hard on the ground.

We head for Longford and arrive at the Abbey Hotel. We get out of the van and I walk straight into a group of nuns who are celebrating a golden jubilee. Quite obviously I am the candidate because I've just stepped out of my own van. I am assuming they have not read the *Irish Daily Mail* and if they have, do not link me with the woman writing an article about the Ryan report which does not flatter the Catholic Church. Not that I couldn't stand by every word I've written but I don't want their jubilee celebrations to end in a row in a car park. I readily recognise that there are plenty of fine men and women in the Catholic Church, many of whom have given a lifetime of service to their community and for small reward. I recognise too that their legacy, in the field of education in particular, is unrivalled. I was educated by nuns and I have said privately and publicly many times that I owe much of who I am to their marvellous education and their enthusiasm for learning in all its guises. However the Church itself – mainly its hierarchy – has been abysmally slow at recognising, apologising and making recompense for the small number of rotten apples in its barrel. That, for me, is the most unforgivable aspect of all of this. I wish the nuns well.

We spend most of the evening talking about the final two weeks, what to do and how to push the campaign on. As ever I am impatient and want to do everything now this minute.

Tea tally: 6

Sunday 24 May

We start early and canvass first Mass in Longford, which is busy. We try not to fall over the charity collection people. Then we head for the cathedral in Athlone, where we stay for the rest of the morning. It's a beautiful day and we get a fairly positive response. I still have mixed feelings about canvassing Mass but I hope that people understand that, under the circumstances, with the constituency being so enormous, we do have to go where lots of people are gathered.

We move to Loughrea and canvass but it's quiet there on Sunday afternoon so we head on for Ennis and are delighted to find it's not raining there this week. There is a fleadh on so there is music everywhere. I get a really warm reception in Ennis again, with lots of recognition and support. After dinner, we sit and listen to some of the impromptu music in the hotel lobby. The great Irish music we've managed to find here and there has been one of the marks of this campaign.

Tea tally: 5

Monday 25 May

We start the day in Clare FM. It's another debate: they are becoming a circuit in a circuit. You never saw these guys (the candidates) in your life before, then you can't stop meeting them. We're on first name terms with their PAs and campaign managers by now! The way the studio is laid out, we are all around the desk and Declan Ganley is on the inside of the desk, again with his own mike. We each get a minute to introduce ourselves. I always hate that especially when you're not first, so you're waiting there to be called. It's a bit like being back in school waiting for your turn to read out an essay or a poem or something! However I now have my new 'statement' to make about the North-West being the engine-driver of the economy. I feel I can say this and believe it and have sufficient examples and evidence to back it up so the leaflet-writing has proven its value. Ganley sounds different today – as if he, too, is tired and has lost his momentum. Perhaps the opinion polls which he constantly denies are true and he is realising that it's hard to go from nowhere and get elected. The debate is well structured and well run by their presenter, John Cooke, who has done his homework and doesn't allow it to descend into chaos.

I challenged Paschal Mooney about Pat the Cope and his only caring about the party and not the country. This is evident in Fianna Fáil's behaviour but, to be honest, you begin to wonder whether people notice or whether they hit the 'Off' button. As with the leaflet, though, you have to fasten your attention on one person in their kitchen, working away while listening to the radio or the guys in the garage, fixing cars with the radio on. People do listen and we are told over and again that many voters don't make their minds up till the last day or even the last minute – so keep going, keep talking, keep persuading. It begins to feel like the end-game now. The tenor of the campaign is changing: it's more urgent, more pressurised. I feel the debate goes well for me and we opt to leave a bit early because we have to get to Galway to do an election programme on RTÉ TV. Better to leave early than arrive late.

It's a quick dash to Galway and a ridiculous run around the docks in the rain and the Volvo chaos to get to the RTÉ interview with Mark Little. I'm on with Pádraig Mac Lochlainn and Declan Ganley, who have also magically appeared from Ennis. It goes well because we get to ask each other a question: I ask DG why he calls his party pan-European when really it isn't and I ask Pádraig why he's running for three seats at the same time. Having done some careful examination of the Libertas statistics I have begun to pick apart this pan-European idea. I don't believe Declan Ganley has real representation across all the countries. I believe the number of candidates is inflated because of the 'list' systems and I know that some of the alliances are nothing more than a flag of convenience for some other party that may have opted for Libertas because it will provide fresh funding. I have been getting some research done to back this up and the figures are not stacking up for Libertas.

Neither of the other candidates answers with huge conviction. Ganley makes the mistake of asking Pádraig and me about what kind of representation we have in Europe. Does he not know how the MEPs sit in Europe and that the Labour Party is part of the PES, the largest block in the European Parliament? He definitely sounds and looks different today – tired and cranky.

We run out of there and out to NUIG and meet Pat Rabbitte, who has very kindly come to canvass with me: NUIG is his alma mater. Michael D and Sabina accompany us so we have the full Labour complement and I am honoured to have them with me. Mags thought we should present a birthday cake to Pat Rabbitte – to celebrate his twenty years in the Dáil and his sixtieth birthday – so I have that pleasure. What a nice thing to do for a decent politician. We've ordered it from Griffins bakers in Shop Street. All the snappers come out – there is something attractive about a cake, which, incidentally none of us ever eats! We do a good canvass of staff in all the canteens with Donncha O'Connell.

Students are finishing their exams and staff are winding down but it's a good canvass.

We go to a shopping centre for a short canvass, then back into Shop Street, which is the heart of the city, and we enjoy the sunshine and a bit of live music and Volvo race atmosphere. We go to the bakers and thank them for the cake. We meet Brian, the Jamaican, who's a mean drummer, and I shake hands with people from around the world. Galway is enjoying the carnival atmosphere: it's a new city, bustling and vibrant and proud of itself.

Then it's into RTÉ radio studio for a *Drivetime with Mary Wilson* debate. They have come to us, which saves us travelling to Dublin. We discuss the Ryan Report and I say it's come up a lot on the doorsteps: that people are angry and sad and disappointed. There's a disbelief when they talk about it; it's not like their anger about the government, it's quite a different reaction. I say that it seems a have taken a long time for us to get to this report as I made the first programme, which was broadcast in 1992. I am reminded that the programme was made in the UK. Yes, it was, and it pointed out that the Catholic Church everywhere routinely moved on child abusers rather than hand them to the authorities, that essentially the Church did not own up to its own problems and was prepared to sacrifice people, especially children, to the preservation of its own image. It took more painful revelations, both in the media – especially by Mary Raftery – and by individuals telling their stories, before the scale of the abuse emerged fully.

There's a bit of a moment when I suggest that the wheels are falling off the Libertas bus because in truth it is not a pan-European party and that at least thirteen countries have no candidates. We're asked not to shout! I agree and do my best but we do have a bit of a laugh when Declan Ganley talks about his private polls showing him taking a seat. Mary Wilson asks him to share the polls and Marian Harkin says she can't afford private polling. She is teased as a well-paid MEP and we all ask Ganley for the polls, which we will never get.

As if we weren't ambitious enough, we now have to drive to Glencolmcille in order to catch the Cancer Bus to Galway. It seemed like a good idea at the time but at seven in the evening in Galway, it's less attractive. Still on we go. Tomorrow is a big day. We drive back across the constituency, discussing the day, the days ahead, whether we have forgotten anything for tomorrow. We get inspiration in the car, call the office and ask the team to print a sheet that says, 'Seat reserved for Mary Harney'. We can stick that on the seat in the morning because, unless I'm a magician, there won't be a minister ready to board a bus in Glencolmcille. We stop for tea on the road – in Gallaghers of Charlestown. Tom has ripped out the kitchen to fit a new one. Does that stop them? Not a bit. It may be 9.30pm but Jody runs off and finds a kettle and a mug and makes me a proper cup of tea. 2,00How kind! Makes it all so worthwhile. We arrive in this beautiful village in west Donegal some time after midnight. Geraldine, our landlady, in Millstone B&B, makes us welcome with tea and a roaring fire, which is such a lovely gesture. Small acts of kindness during a campaign make such a difference. I think exhaustion is the word that conjures our state at this point. I also suspect that Glencolmcille haven't had too many Labour Party campaigners in the past.

We have had to miss the Carers' Association meeting in Castlerea tonight. They want MEPs to lobby for the official census to include a question on carers in all EU member states – Ireland already has this question – and to heed the rights of carers in the Working Time Directive Opt-out clause. Roscommon apparently has the highest number of carers in the country and I'm sorry we can't attend.

In the post a survey from Berlin: the European Parliament Election Candidate Study from the European University Institute. There are more logos on the top of the page of supporting organisations and associations than I've had hot dinners on this campaign. It's not the first survey. It's the strange underbelly side of the campaign: all the people and organisations that come out of the woodwork asking questions and asking for your support in the form of pledges which are then forwarded to various organisations. The amount of paperwork and e-paperwork it generates serves as a reminder of how small our team is and how hard we work to keep on top of everything.

Tea tally: 8

Tuesday 26 May

We are up early so I can do some radio interviews about the Cancer Bus. It's glorious and what better place to wake up? A good breakfast gets us motivated. Pat and Kristen have arrived from Sligo, complete with Lily McMorrow and Caitríona McGoldrick from the Cancer Services Campaign. They are prepared to travel the journey. The Minister for Health has failed to materialise. We do lots of photos and set off on the bus while David drives the van. Spirits are high because we are doing something and it matters. On the way we stop and pick up cancer survivor Marian Murrin and her friend Una Erskine.

We get to Donegal town and are met by another group of protestors. I have now discovered that the soap box, due to make its début today, has been left on the side of the road in Glencolmcille. I improvise a platform on a bench in the Diamond in Donegal and don't care if people think I'm mad. Let's face it: what's happening with the cancer services is quite mad, so I how could I be madder! I have to say that the road to Donegal is poor – bumpy, twisty and narrow – and although I am a good traveller and have obviously travelled much during this campaign, on this bus I feel decidedly nauseous and am glad to stop. I know that the women aren't enjoying it either and Caitríona is emotional because it reminds her of the daily trundling up and down to Galway which she did last year (2008) from her home in Coolaney, south Sligo. Because she has a young daughter she opted to do the journey for radiotherapy every day. She recalled one very hot day on the bus when the air conditioning was broken and it felt like she was burning inside: that, combined with the heat on the bus, was unbearable. On other days, she would be on the bus before the hospital would phone to say the machine was broken down and that there would be no treatment that day!

We arrive in Sligo General, where there's a great welcome. Lots of people and journalists have turned up to encourage us. We've been keeping a clock on the travelling time and already it's two hours. I can't imagine how it would feel to do this journey on your own, feeling ill, maybe on a Monday to go to Galway for a week's treatment. The stress of this kind of treatment can't help people who are very ill already. Back on the bus and on to Galway. When we arrive there is quite a good crowd from the party to meet us. We feel we've been through a lot, just doing that journey, and I know the women have to do the journey back again.

People asked if it was worth it, especially when I knew the Minister would never come. Of course it was worth it. If you are fighting a cause, you have to keep finding new ways of drawing attention to that cause and it's quite in order to point out that the people who draw up the 'rules' for how patients are treated are themselves never treated this way. If I was working as a journalist in Africa and I came upon this story about sick people from rural areas being shuttled by bus for long distances on poor roads, I would write about it to expose their plight. Well, welcome to third-world services in Ireland's North-West! The total driving time is four hours and forty minutes. While we are there, a young woman is leaving hospital in a wheelchair. She seems very ill. We talk to the people who are with her and they tell us that she is twenty-one and has cancer and is going home for a couple of days of respite care. I wonder why they look so distraught and it transpired that the hospital had told them it cannot guarantee a bed for her when she comes back on Friday!

Mags urges me to eat something; I get distracted and upset about things and forget to.

Exhausted. Drive to Mullingar Park Hotel.

Tea tally: 7

Wednesday 27 May

Set off for Longford early. Send a congratulations fax to my daughter Grace who is receiving a Texaco Art Award today. Not quite the same as being there with her.

Today is definitely media day. Do they conspire to set us an impossible obstacle course? I wonder. No, it just feels like it and again it underlines the size of the constituency and the wealth of local radio and how seriously they take the elections. We start in Longford with Pádraig Mac Lochlainn and Joe O'Reilly for a short debate, more manageable because there are only three of us. Joe looks tired today. Then we head for Galway for one of the most important debates, on Galway Bay. FM. It's hosted by Keith Finnegan, who has damaged his back, so has to stand up to run the show. It's in a good big room: there is space for everyone and everyone has come.

I am amazed by an early intervention from Paschal Mooney when he tells me specifically that he can offer a guarantee that the Western Rail Corridor will go ahead. I ask him if he is a messenger boy for the Minister for Transport, Noel Dempsey. He says that it is guaranteed. There is a heated exchange with Declan Ganley about the amount of legislation that is passed by Europe and we all pile in. I've taken the trouble to read Sinn Féin's document 'Awakening the West', with which Pádraig Mac Lochlainn was involved, and I say to him that it's the most pessimistic document I have ever read that's supposed to be about economic regeneration: a list of all the shortcomings rather than the can-dos. In the main, I think the debate goes well and am happy when I have to leave a bit early to drive to Dublin for *Tonight with Vincent Browne*. Not exactly what one might wish to do at 8 in the evening but we're nothing if not determined and off we go. Of course we've discussed it – Joe and Pádraig and independent Michael will be there. We know we are the outsiders but we never say that. We have to perform and remember there are still people looking for someone to vote for.

It's a mad dash and I get cross when we get lost at the very end: there are no signs for TV3 and it's in an industrial estate and I'm tired. Fortunately it's fairly rare for me to get cross. I change my clothes when we get there, get make-up and we're in studio. I've never been on with Vincent before but we know each other from of old, when he was editor of the *Sunday Tribune* and I was freelance. He was known as 'Mad Dog Browne' and there were sparks and clashes all the time, although not with me because I was only ever passing through. My memory of him is of a journalist who wanted to throw brickbats at government and who was never afraid to ask tough questions and be cynical about politics and the political process. Quite healthy, really. I have a memory of writing a story for the *Sunday Tribune,* about a man who had contracted HIV from contaminated blood and was dying. I remember sitting in his bedroom talking to him and wondering how this could happen and why nobody would be held accountable for his death.

Unfortunately Europe is not Vincent's favourite subject so he's not going to give anyone an easy time. He gives me a hard time for describing the work of an MEP as 'donkey work' – which is actually true. I think MEPs have little influence individually; it's a very collaborative, collegiate process and involves a lot of reading and meetings and the capacity to have influence within your group or party. Vincent gives Pádraig a hard time about the IRA's record of 'killing children'. It was a hard day and we are tired at a new level. I write a letter to Mary Harney's office describing the bus journey and wonder if I will ever have a reply.

Dear Mr Scully

I would be grateful if you would forward the following to Minister Harney.

I made the journey from Glencolmcille in County Donegal to Galway as promised. The journey took four hours and forty minutes. Four women travelled with me. Three of these had suffered from cancer and had had to use the 'Cancer Bus'. Two of them, Lily and Caitríona, had not had to travel from Glencolmcille, so they travelled from Sligo to Glencolmcille to accompany us because they felt it would help their understanding of the issue!

I am never car-sick and I came pretty close yesterday morning in Donegal, because the road is so bad. And I am not ill. Our bus was very similar to the usual bus – nineteen seats, quite hard. The difference was that ours had no toilet and was slightly smaller than the usual bus but there were only six of us on the bus. Often, especially on Mondays and Fridays, the nineteen seats are full of ill people.

The women's stories, as told on the bus, were simply unbelievable and, coming from me, someone who has heard a huge range of stories over the years, that's pretty strong language. They talked of the indignity of having no choice but to use the toilet on the bus, pretty much in front of everyone. They talked about the older men, especially older farmers, looking lost and confused, many of them never having spent time away from home and certainly not away from home while being ill.

They talked about travelling in the summer when the air conditioning on the bus was broken and it was 30°C outside and in. If you are having radiotherapy your skin often burns and blisters and this causes enormous pain. Caitríona said you can't nod off on the bus because you might lean on someone else and hurt them. She ended up having to take her wig off on the bus because it was so hot.

And, sometimes someone wants to get off the bus because they feel ill and can't because the driver has a schedule and has to keep going. And the men with prostate cancer have to queue for the toilet.

Patient Tony Burke joined us at University College Hospital Galway. He is having radiotherapy at the moment and is a bus driver himself. He has given up taking the bus because he couldn't bear it; too stressful and too uncomfortable.

These people talk about the upset of 'commuting' on a daily basis from Sligo for treatment and the loneliness of being away from family for a week at a time if they have to stay in Galway, then having to face a horrendous journey back after five days of treatment. And the radiotherapy machines are often broken or having maintenance work so the weeks of travelling are extended because of this and the stress for everyone is increased. Oh, and there are people who never make the journey at all because they are too old. So they don't get the treatment and they die!

And, finally when we were standing at the hospital, a

woman from Offaly came over to explain that she had come to the hospital to help her neighbours drive home their twenty-year old daughter for a couple of days for a break from hospital. The young woman has spine cancer and needs treatment and was told as she got into the car that the hospital could not guarantee that there would be a bed for her on Friday. The family, the woman and the neighbours were distraught and that's on top of watching this beautiful young woman suffer intense pain and discomfort.

We all wanted you to be there. Even if you were too busy, perhaps you could have sent a representative from among the many people in your department. Your absence and the lack of debate on the matter leaves people of the North-West feeling abandoned – and they are right to be. This treatment of these patients will continue into the future under your plan for centres of excellence and your plan will not bring excellence to them.

Redrawing the plan to include the thousands of people who live in the North-West would not be a crime or a weakness. It's never too late to adopt a common-sense approach and to show humanity.

Yours sincerely

Tea tally: 8

Thursday 28 May

Mags arrives early to my room but we are slow today and don't leave Dublin until after 11. Back to Galway. It's a conscious decision, to spend more time there: I begin to feel I live on Shop Street. I am down today; I feel I messed up Vincent Browne because of the 'donkey work' thing and also because it appears I got some little thing wrong about the Lisbon Treaty. It has shaken my confidence so Mags decides on a treat and insists I stay in the Meyrick tonight so I can just crash in comfort. It's a wall moment; the tiredness is sapping my resilience and begins to make me feel a bit mad. The Hothouse Flowers play tonight for the Volvo, which reminds me that the world is going on all round me in its normal circuit. I am in some different internal loop which occasionally intersects with the real world; really it's quite weird.

I receive a letter from the Knights of Columbanus asking if I were elected and there was a vote in the European Parliament whether I would 'support any proposals enabling euthanasia'. I confess I never replied. There is correspondence too from the Irish Retailers, the Consumers' Association, the National Federation of Voluntary Bodies, the Irish Pharmacy Union and Birdwatch Ireland. Being a public representative or standing to become one means you are answerable to people in every shape, form, alliance, group they choose. And there are a lot of them!

Tea tally: 5

Friday 29 May

The first day of the last week and we keep moving. I enjoy a constructive breakfast with Proinsias to talk about the Lisbon Treaty, to make sure I get it right the next time. He has kindly come to Galway to launch a Safer Streets Initiative with me in the Rape Crisis Centre. I am touched that, as another candidate, he would make time to come and support me. It's a good subject and an important one as women increasingly feel vulnerable on our streets and there are very simple cost-effective steps that councils could take to make streets more attractive. Proinsias has long had an interest in equality and women's issues and pressed successfully for the Lisbon Treaty to pledge to policies that would 'combat all kinds of domestic violence' and that member states would take all measures to 'prevent and punish these criminal acts and to support and protect the victims'. It's a subject most people would not see Europe as contributing to because it never gets any publicity. I'm glad to be able to add my voice, in a small way, to such an important matter.

We chase from Galway to Mullingar to meet Eamon Gilmore and his entourage. I really haven't got to grips with this bit of the campaign. I understand it and appreciate it but have not really worked out how to do it right when there are so many of us. We grab a sandwich and a cup of tea in a garage in Mullingar and pick up with the others. We are with Willy Penrose and his gang and we do a walkabout with RTÉ in Mullingar, then on to Athlone. Then it's on to Galway.

I am scheduled to do Newstalk but get caught in really bad traffic. We have to argue quite strongly with them when they threaten not to let me contribute because I am not in studio. We stand our ground and get on air. Inevitably we talk about the traffic in Galway and I advocate the GLUAS, which Frank Fahey confuses with the Luas, so there's a bit of a ding-dong. We arrive in time for one of the high points – the party leader's tour of the

Green Dragon boat. It's a stunning evening in Galway and the quays are thronged with people. We climb down into the *Green Dragon* with skipper Ian Walker. It is quite amazing. It's not really a boat – it's a racing vessel which makes a nod to the needs of the crew. The sleeping and eating arrangements are very basic and I can see that only the fittest and the most dedicated would survive this. My opinion of the sport soars in five minutes because I confess to being a landlubber who enjoys the seaside when there's ice cream and sunshine. The idea of having to cope with the sea up close and very personal is not in my comfort zone so I will look at these guys in a whole new light from now on.

We head for Shop Street and canvass with Eamon. It goes better this time. I am getting better at it and it's a Friday and sunny and people are feeling kind. There is a pause then and some muttering and phone calls and I don't know what's happening. There is debate and discussion about whether Eamon should go back to Dublin as planned or stay in Claregalway. We go back to the cars, then Mags tells me the latest opinion polls are out. I am down to 5 per cent. I know now what the muttering is about and I see that Mags had the hardest job – having to tell me when she knows how it will affect me. Timing is everything, as ever, and I react badly. I take it personally and wonder what is the point of all the effort. I started as an outsider and will finish as one and all the effort will go for nought. The rational side of my brain tells me it's nonsense, that I always knew I would be an outsider and that there were other good reasons for standing.

Tiredness prevails and I can't shake off the disappointment to be down 1 per cent at this stage and to feel like a lost cause. There is a week to go and it will be hard to galvanise myself now with that figure as my guiding light. The party comes to the rescue and Eamon rows in with support and sound advice. He has stayed for that reason, even though it means he will have to get up extra early tomorrow to get back. We have dinner and a glass of wine. He talks about polls, about elections, about getting elected, about how hard it is in this constituency, how much Irish politics still relies on the handshake and the smile and it's hard to do that with nearly a million people. Perhaps I have crossed a Rubicon here: understanding now what voters are like and knowing what it's like to put myself out there and be rejected; believing that I have new things to say and a new approach but realising that people will continue to support the 'team' they always supported, that it takes a long time for people to accept a new face and change. I won't say it's not hard. It's very hard.

Tea tally: 4

Saturday 30 May

A whole day in Galway. Summer has arrived and it's glorious. We leave Claregalway and drive in and, yes, it's time for Shop Street one more time. Thronged. Am not having a good day: still down after the poll and can't galvanise myself. Too tired, I guess, and I feel the mountain getting higher. But I ring L and have a laugh and some encouragement from outside the bubble, then C sends a really good text with eight reasons to ignore the poll and he's right:

1. Candidates with lower levels of support are under-counted in opinion polls.
2. Labour's support is continuing to rise.

3. Support is accurate to +-3 per cent on average, more margin of error in case of smaller parties, so the poll is consistent with your support being higher now than it was last time
4. The day you decided to stand, if you were asked if you'd be satisfied to poll (statistically) level with the second FF-er what would you have said? That's where you are now.
5. There's still a week to go.
6. Never has Ireland needed able public-spirited candidates more than today.
7. You will attract more transfers than Number Ones and you only need to poll a few points to be around for a cascade of transfers.
8. For the next election what matters is how you poll in Sligo.

It makes me smile even if it's not all true and it's hugely thoughtful of him to put all that into a text so I manage to shake off the gloom and reapply energy and make-up. On the streets, there's lots of support. We go to Salthill and it's really hot. Meet my daughter Roberta with her friend Hilary. She tells me that seeing me wearing all white with sunglasses and flanked by two 'minders' somehow makes her think of Michael Jackson! I have a drink – it should have been a gin after that comment – then she goes for the bus and we carry on to canvass at Masses with Michael D and Sabina. Then a break and back out to hear Sharon Shannon, which is just lovely. What a stunning musician and what a great atmosphere. We go into one of the tents to have a drink and enjoy some amazing Volvo cakes, designed, I think, by the bakers who designed Pat's cake. They've been busy this week. Meet my oldest friend in the world, Cathy, and her husband Brian, and again it's great to see non-campaign people. Sabina has kindly agreed that we can stay at hers and her warmth and welcome are great. Somehow Mags and I, despite the late hour, turn to the future and beyond the election. We have managed not to talk about this at all during the campaign and our discussion now has been precipitated by the opinion polls and by the 'endgame' feel in the air. Of course there are no answers; there couldn't be when we can' t really think straight.

Tea tally: 5

Sunday 31 May

A gorgeous summer's day. What a joy: easy to wear summer clothes. People are easier; we are easier. We are all up early to have breakfast before we canvass the churches. Idly I wonder how many times Michael D has done this. After all, he's been forty years in politics so his car must know its own way to the best spots to canvass. It's very easy with Michael D. Everyone knows him, stops and shakes hands with him and wishes me luck. As we stand under a tree to shelter from the noonday sun I ask him what keeps him going: is it the cause? 'It's the conviction,' he says simply. 'It's what matters.' Sometimes he can be exceptionally eloquent and enjoys the words for the sheer pleasure they afford. Sometimes he opts for directness. I think about conviction as we smile at people and wave as they leave the car park and I wonder at his forty years of caring and believing – and here he is working hard for me, as is Sabina, who has gone to another few churches because there are too many of us. It's been a good morning and I appreciate everyone's help, although I can feel the pressure mounting a bit as we are into countdown territory now.

We have to make decisions about the last few days and the words of party organisers much earlier on in the campaign come back to haunt me. 'Labour loses it in the last week. You need to plan for it, you need to have money to spend, you need to bring on something new.' We have talked about it but have never nailed anything down and we're not going to now. I'm keen to get a big wagon in Mullingar – a bandwagon – and get one person from each county in the constituency to climb on it: the people the government has let down in this recession – a farmer, a special needs teacher, a traveller child…the list would be longer than eleven but that would be a start. But I feel already that the project is beyond us: we don't have enough people to do it, to galvanise it, simply to make it happen. And I will get too stressed and stretched. We don't agree not to; we just park it. We do have some great new posters though, me with Michael D for Galway, me with Willie Penrose for Mullingar and me with Eamon Gilmore for Sligo. We talk about maybe going back to Donegal on Wednesday but we're not sure. Would we be better in Sligo? I suspect that the party will pour its resources into Leinster and Munster, the places where we are most likely to make gains. That's hard to accept that but it's the right decision for the party. Two extra seats is worth fighting for and you always have to focus your energies where you think you will win.

It's time to say goodbye to Galway for the last time. It's been great and I'm honoured to have had the time there, especially to enjoy the Volvo and the enormous goodwill and enthusiasm in the city. All the councillors and candidates have been generous, as have Michael D and his family. Theirs is a good machine and they have worked hard for such a long time so it's very special. We climb into the bus and head for Kilbeggan to meet my cousins at the races. I haven't been to the Kilbeggan Races since I was a teenager; I remember the donkey derby and the candy floss but now I don't know quite what to expect. I read in the *Sunday Tribune* on the way up the road that Libertas has spent €900,000 on the European elections in Ireland, although Declan Ganley has denied this. Whatever the truth of the Libertas spend, it's a whole lot higher than our diet of scones and tea and one small bus with my face on it. The Libertas posters were plastered everywhere across the country and I stood in Dublin one day and counted ten buses around me, all with Libertas advertisements. There's a row about stolen posters too, which apparently is one of the headaches of postering. I don't think we've noticed any of ours going but I'm not counting!

The sun continues to shine; in fact it's quite glorious. We canvass outside the races as people go in. There's quite a big crowd and Marian Harkin's people are just behind us. It turns out that she is at the GAA match our Sligo canvassers are at; it's always interesting to see where the other candidates turn up. We feel a bit naked after Galway but then we go inside and enjoy a 'soft canvass', talking to the cousins and meeting their friends and neighbours, some of whom I remember from a very long time ago. There are more cousins there than I thought there would be and it's great to make contact again after such a long time. Quite a number of people have seen me with Vincent Browne and most are critical of how grumpy and cynical he was with me. We have tea and wander again, then it's time to place a few bets, which naturally we lose. It's strange to be here too and it has changed from my memory of it. It's bigger now with stands and naturally a donkey-free zone. This is post Celtic Tiger racing, not as it used to be: just a bit of fun for locals.

We drive to Cavan. On the way we stop briefly at beautiful Lake Mullagh. The sun is shining and there are adults and kids enjoying the moment. As we stand and watch, a woman says she saw me with Vincent Browne and how cranky he was and how well I did! There is no escaping the campaign unless you lock yourself in a room. We meet up with Liam Hogan and his wife Mary G. and Councillor Des Cullen. They are having a fundraiser. The pub is full and noisy and very hot. Fundraisers are hard work and necessary. They're not aimed at raising a fortune – this is not the Galway tent, after all. It's usually friends and family who come out to enjoy an evening of music or a race evening or pub quiz. We say hello to a few people, then leave. We're tired – it's been a twelve-hour day on show. We stay in the Cavan Crystal. I still have work to do for *Prime Time* and *The Late Debate*.

We still haven't definitely decided to go to Donegal but my feeling is that we will. Party HQ think we shouldn't go because it's too far and there are very few votes there but I feel strongly that we should go, without quite knowing why: maybe it's the few texts of support I've had from there and the people I do know there asking me to go. Feel badly too for never getting to Achill. All the beautiful summers I spent there; it's been part of our family life for such a long time and there's even a cow called Roberta there somewhere, if she's still standing! We really meant to: we just never made the extra stretch.

Tea tally: 4

Monday 1 June

It really is the very last week – it's June and the moments are slipping away. We do a door-knock with our Cavan-town candidate, Liam Hogan, which is quite productive, if short, and we meet Peggy Brady, who must be Ireland's oldest barwoman, and have a cup of tea with her. We end up today in the Cavan jamboree, which is literally in the middle of nowhere, in Killinkere. It's hot and noisy and not a great place to canvass, as it turns out. We do have a great photo op – with the Connacht He-Men, who lift me with the greatest of ease as their normal challenge is lifting cars and if I lose any more weight on this campaign, I will disappear. I talk to head office about the last few days and whether we ought to have a public voting strategy; all this while the hen race takes place at the jamboree, with the final winner 'Henny Penny'. All I know is that my hens will run very fast if they think there's food in the offing. Otherwise they prefer a bit of dust-bathing. We drive on for Carrickmacross. On the way I get out to help a farmer, John Cooney, with his cows. It's a beautiful sunny evening – the rural idyll. What brings reality check is the farmer's own story about milk prices and the €100 he reckons he's losing every day he gets out of bed. Although I am familiar with the story and have talked about it, it is always sobering to see it in front of you: to see the face, to hear the anger and the sorrow. This man wants to farm but at the rate he's going, he will be forced off the land. Can MEPs fix this problem? I'm not sure, and I have tried by talking to various specialists in farming to get an answer, a proposal, a solution to the milk price problem, but I have to say I have yet to be convinced that anyone knows the answer – apart from intervening in the market, which is easy to say, so much harder to do.

We have arranged to meet our Monaghan colleagues in the bar and it's all I can do to drag myself downstairs. I feel really tired and anxious about tomorrow's *Prime Time*. I know it's important to be there and to do well and, again, I have that feeling of preparing without knowing what the questions might be. I have drawn up a shortlist of queries which I want our party strategy people to help me with for tomorrow: things that have come up over and again or questions to which I never quite knew the answer!

Tea tally: 6

Tuesday 2 June

Thankfully another sunny morning and the canvass in Carrick goes well. We do the high street fairly methodically and there is quite good recognition and quite a lot of people telling their stories, which for me is the best part of a canvass – when you can listen to what people want to say. A Garda stops me and strikes up a conversation which begins something like, 'You're brave enough to be out on the street then?' I am completely thrown by this and my mind immediately begins to race to see if I have said something about the Gardaí, the town, something outrageous – or did someone else in the Labour Party say something that I missed. In a three-second period I can think of nothing, so I try to continue smiling while I wait for his next insult. Instead he tells me about the Taoiseach's arrival in the town the previous evening when the festival was on and people's curiosity as to why he did not come out canvassing. Well, indeed! It was a strange way of paying a compliment but we take them where we can. I know my friend Lynne from Manchester has taken my children canvassing in Tubbercurry and Ballymote. I know too that that's what we needed all along – more bodies. It's teamwork with as many as you can muster.

We leave Carrick and head for Dublin and a long and very useful briefing ahead of tonight's TV. I find the strange thing about television in relation to the campaign is that it reaches such a large audience which is invisible at the time of the appearance. Normally shaking hands or speaking at a conference or debate, I get to see who I'm talking to: it's quite a different skill, speaking to the invisible as if they are visible.

After the briefing, my brain is crammed again so Mags and I head for a hotel for some food and to do the inevitable 'what to wear' moment. Even though we had already decided, we have to decide all over again! Fortunately we can leave make-up to RTÉ, who always do a great job. We arrive with about the right amount of time. I get lost coming back out of make-up, which is pretty stupid, and find my way back to the green room just in time! In studio, Mark Little explains how the show will run and reminds us not to talk over one another.

It goes fine, I think. I sit next to Eoin Ryan, who knows how much pressure he is under for his seat, then Joe Higgins, who is replaced by Ray O'Malley for Libertas. Sinn Féin's Mary Lou McDonald is over the far side and also under extreme pressure; the calmest one is Colm Burke from Fine Gael. Looking back I realise that Joe is the only one on that panel who won a seat! However I am much calmer this time round and can only conclude that practice helps and also that the game is nearly over and there is only so much more that can be achieved. I criticise Ray O'Malley when he raises the question of legislation being rushed through Europe. I ask him how he would know that as he's never been there!

I criticise Eoin Ryan too. Then it's over and time for bed. I write a blog before sleep. I find calling it 'Stories from the Frontline' is a good way for the journalist in me to respond to the political.

Tea tally: 7

Wednesday 3 June

If we get up any earlier, it will be yesterday. Goodness knows why we decided to go to Donegal but this indeed is what we do. Just trying to check our stamina, perhaps. So off we go at the crack of dawn to Moville. Could we go any further north?

Of course it's the day the Leaving and Junior Cert exams start so we are taking extra care not to play our music too loudly. Yes, we now have 'Vote Susan O'Keeffe, a courageous voice in Europe' blaring from the top of our bus, complete with music – it makes me smile every time we put it on. OK, laugh out loud; my friend R recorded it for me and I think he was laughing too. I wonder what the voters are thinking. We chose KT Tunstall's 'Suddenly I See' as 'my' election song – I like it. It was a toss-up between that and U2's 'Beautiful Day' which we put on the election tape. Sometimes we play 'Suddenly I See' in the car, really loudly, and I sing along – that probably wouldn't help my canvassing very much:

> *Suddenly I see (Suddenly I see)*
> *This is what I wanna be*
> *Suddenly I see (Suddenly I see)*
> *Why the hell it means so much to me*

We have a cup of tea in Moville with our candidate Martin Farren and his campaign manager Jim. We canvass in the town, then head for a community meeting with Martin. They're good people and we have a useful discussion. Then off to Raphoe to meet Frank McBrearty Junior, who is standing in the local election for the first time. Despite spending a long time producing the RTÉ documentary about Donegal publican Frank Shortt, I have never met the McBreartys. Frank won €1.5 million in the High Court for malicious prosecution as well as wrongful and false arrest. I have met Frank at other functions but not in his home patch. We do a canvass with him – he knows everyone in the town – then we head for Lifford. I realise I've never been there, even though my parents lived there many moons ago when my father was county manager. It's time to head for Sligo. We have team dinner – a very rare moment indeed – then I head to RTÉ Sligo for the *Late Debate*. This really is the last hurrah. Paschal Mooney is in the Athlone studio, Jim Higgins is in Galway, economist Jim Power and analyst Nick Coffey are in studio in Dublin. I feel totally at ease: sometimes it's easier when you have the studio all to yourself and also it is the last time and the die is probably pretty much cast at this stage. Two things happen at the very end of the show: Jim and Nick both say it would be good to see me doing well in the North-West. That is the first time anyone has said anything of this kind in the whole campaign and it's a good way to end. Then, as Rachel English is winding up, she thanks her studio guests and the 'politicians': 'Jim Higgins, Paschal Mooney and Susan O'Keeffe'. No one has called me that out loud in public before and it seems strange to know that I am now considered one.

Tea tally: 6

Thursday 4 June

It's the last day really. The sun is shining and Mags and I with our posters canvass the traffic going in and out of Sligo town at the top of Pearse Street. It's good fun and people are good-humoured. The lorry drivers honk their horns and some people wave. We spend the rest of the day in town, doing a gentle canvass, with the family. Eight-year old Eva is good at smiling at people and handing out leaflets; she seems to hand out more than any of us. Everyone has pitched in to help so we look busy. It's odd to be in Sligo on an ordinary shopping day with a completely different hat on and with people coming over and wishing me well. Many people say they'll give their Number One to Marian Harkin and their Number Two to me and that's to be expected – this is Marian's stronghold and she has worked hard here over the years. I have huge respect for her. Although I am certain never to be able to use her Number Twos, it's good to know people are happy to give me their second preference. We drink more cups of tea, in Lyons Warehouse and Café Fleur and finally the children persuade me to eat so we are very European and sit in the sun outside Bistro Bianconi and have pizza. I get texts of good wishes from friends and some flowers arrive at home. Mags leaves to drive south to vote in Thomastown. We go home and flop. Nothing left to do.

Tea tally: 7

Friday 5 June

The day has arrived. It feels very unreal. Grace, Lynne, Kirsten and I battle a very windy cool morning at the traffic lights on the north side of Sligo. The weather has turned and we're worried that it might rain, which is never good on polling day. We have posters at the various lines of traffic and survive for about an hour: it's quite cold but we get quite a lot of recognition. People smile and give the thumbs-up. Mags phones to say she is late arriving because she couldn't find the polling station in Thomastown – they moved it so she spent twenty minutes driving round looking for it at 7 in the morning! We have tea and make our way to Ballisodare to vote. I wanted to wait for Mags to be there – it seemed right! We meet in Ballisodare – Mags has picked Pat up en route and Paul brings the children and Lynne. We also have a bit of trouble finding the polling station: it's a school in a housing estate. We take some silly photos outside and as we go in we meet my neighbour, Michael L., who tells me he got the 7am train from Dublin to vote for me! Now that is dedication as he also has to go back on the train. Some people really do treat their right to vote very seriously. We take photos inside too. As I can't find my glasses I have to put in the numbers without them! Eva stands with me and keeps me on the straight and narrow. It really is the weirdest moment: putting the Number 1 next to myself and defying the nuns' counsel that you should never vote for yourself! Paul votes too and I almost forget that the children can't. They've been so generous and contributed so much that it seems right they should be able to vote. We go and have lunch in the Teeling Café in Collooney. Then back into town and out to Drumcliffe: after all I did promise Mags she would have a chance to see Yeats's grave during the campaign and I like to keep my word. Then back to town and more tea. It's such a strange day. It's about being visible but not really campaigning. I've almost forgotten what to do. Mags takes a fit and we drive to Longford – for fish and chips. Now that *is* funny. I guess that was her one opportunity to eat what we have managed to avoid for almost the entire campaign. Our local candidate, Seamus Co, joins us for a cup of tea. We walk up and down the main street, call it a day and drive home. There's nothing more to be done now. The game is over. At least the weather seemed to hold up round the country.

Tea tally: 9

Saturday 6 June

Our count won't start till tomorrow but we know that there will be some tallying today. The turnout yesterday was almost 59 per cent, as against the European average of 43 per cent. It was higher in the North-West than anywhere else, at 63 per cent. We have breakfast; then in the early afternoon, I drive into town to meet Mags at the local count. We move between the two locations. Alwyn Love is anxious. Marcella McGarry is elected and is delighted, as she should be: it's her first time to run. Our outgoing mayor, Veronica Cawley, does well and is re-elected, as is Councillor Jimmy McGarry. Their hard work and perseverance have paid off and they go to celebrate. It's a very odd day – a sort of in-between waiting kind of day. The exit polls suggest I'm on 8 per cent but they are rarely right for the Europeans so we have to take them with a grain of salt. I go home but find I am too anxious to be in the real world when I still belong in unreal territory. Mags and I drive to Castlebar. We arrive at Days Hotel, a strange place which has a row of mirrors in the lobby that make one feel drunk when completely sober. We join the Harkin people, then some of Jim Higgins's team shows up too. By now some of the results are in from round the country and it's clear already that the government has taken a hit and that Labour has made gains in Dublin but sadly not in either by-election. Ivana Bacik and Alex White will be disappointed, especially Alex, as he has worked so hard over the last while, only to lose to George Lee. We stay late: it seems the only thing to do. Normal time has been suspended. Although I know I won't be elected, the anxiety about not letting the side down is greater than I thought it would be and it's difficult to return to normality.

Sunday 7 June

Mags and I get to the count in the Royal Event Centre pretty much as it opens, so we can get our precious passes. We have a brief look and run away for breakfast at the hotel. We see other teams preparing for the long day and we know there will be no early declaration. The turnout was high: nearly half a million votes to count. We go back over: I'm very curious. Of course I've been to counts before, here and in the UK, but it's different when you're a candidate. You're not looking for the story; you *are* the story. Ocean FM grab me to do a quick interview and I'm happy to oblige as they are stuck early in the morning for a bit of colour and someone new to talk to. I know that feeling. So I sit up high and talk about the piles of ballot papers, which are quite staggering. Then I'm asked to predict the seats and that's a hard moment but I say, 'Status quo,' with Pat the Cope being Seán Ó Neachtain.

I do another interview with Newstalk and don't change my position. Of course I know what they want to hear – they would like the story to be Libertas getting elected because then the count would really hot up and the constituency would be the centre of the whole election. As a journalist I understand that but I'm happy to believe our understanding on the ground all along and our intuition that Declan Ganley will not be elected. We go back to the hotel and have a bit of a rest, which ends up with me starting on my diary piece for the *Irish Daily Mail*. I find that I'm not inclined to sleep. I talk for a while to Kathy Sheridan from *The Irish Times* and explain what it was like to have Libertas be the story of the campaign when in fact the wheels fell off the Libertas bus very early on.

The family arrives with Anne and Lynne and David. We can get them into the count in relays because we don't have quite enough passes. That's everyone's problem, really, although I think Marian Harkin's crew stole a clever march and got some from independents Michael McNamara and Fiachra Ó Luain. By now all the candidates are around the place, coming and going. Then a nice surprise: Mark and Neil and Karen arrive from party HQ in Dublin, Neil complete with dyed red hair. It makes me laugh a lot, which is no bad thing. There is an atmosphere of waiting, although we know it will be a while yet, and there is much phoning and texting about the other candidates. I realise the children are all hungry so we go to the dining room next door which is turning out food – it's just about edible but it's not a moment for haute cuisine. Then back to the count with the usual: will it be now or in ten minutes?'

We manage with some subterfuge to get all of us in for the declaration. Nobody is elected on the first count, which is normal. I get 28,708 first preferences and we cheer. I am pleased and everyone else is even more pleased than me. Labour has never ever got so many votes in this constituency before. And even better, Declan Ganley doesn't look like he's got enough votes either. When it comes to the second count, the Ganley machine throws a spanner in the works. A two-hour long conversation with the returning officer ensues, by which stage it is nearly midnight. No one is really surprised by this but it means the count is abandoned as the returning officer decides to run a recheck – which is almost like a recount but not in quite as much detail.

What is really lovely is the number of gracious handshakes I receive from the other teams, especially Marian's people. I'm surprised by the warmth and the immediate encouragement that I should run again, in a general election. I had not anticipated this at all. I don't know what it means and fortunately I don't have to try to work it out. I go over and hug Marian and congratulate Jim and Joe. Sinn Féin's Pádraig Mac Lochlainn runs out, possibly to get to Donegal to see if he is elected to the County Council. (He is.) He never reappears. He must be disappointed as he hasn't repeated the success the party had the last time with Pearse Doherty.

The family leaves. Declan Ganley is on the radio saying he will get loads of transfers from…me! I find that hard to believe. No one else is happy, apart from the journalists, who smell a story. There is much confusion as to what has happened or why the recheck has been demanded. There are suggestions of missing votes. It's time for a glass of wine, so we retire to the mad mirror lobby where Declan Ganley's children are variously sitting down, running round or popping up to watch their dad on television. I end up chucking half a glass of wine all over Neil – and it's not because I've been drinking. It was the first glass! We stay up late, chatting, watching television, winding down our own campaign, really, wanting to know how the others are getting on around the country and wondering what's happening at our own count. Marian Harkin topped the poll. And it looks like Higgins and

Gallagher will get in, unless something very odd happens with the transfers. Proinsias and Nessa will get elected. Alan's position is not at all clear. We retire. It's been a long, long day. I'm happy we did a good job. Sleep comes very quickly.

Monday 8 June
It's another waiting day, waiting anxiously to hear the story of the missing votes. Did someone put a bundle of votes in the wrong pile? Were they put in the wrong bin? Will Ganley's first preferences soar? I'm not there first thing but I hear later that he was apparently in talking to the counters before they started for the day, in the presence of the returning office. There is much annoyance around the place as counts in other constituencies are proceeding and we are stalled. There is a recount in Dublin too. I write more of my article and we turn to wondering whether we might get our deposit back! Now that would be a first. I need just over 2000 transfers from the others who were eliminated. But we have to wait to see what's next. There is still a lot of warmth and encouragement for me and I continue to find that strange. Strange nice. I guess we spent a long time competing and now we're not competing any longer. Not that I was ever going to cause them a problem, but I had to compete as if I would.

Finally we get news that an announcement is due – about 5pm. Well, who would have guessed it? Yes there were missing votes – 3000 – that were given to Declan Ganley and should have been given to Fiachra Ó Luain. There is cheering and clapping. His recount has resulted in a loss. They find fifty missing votes for me too so I'm happy and because the missing votes go to Fiachra they are now available to be transferred – some to me – so it ups the chances of me getting my deposit back. We go away and everyone enjoys the moment: even the counters are smiling now.

I finish writing my piece for the *Irish Daily Mail* on what it feels like to have been the candidate. It's quite useful to stop and think about it in a formal way.

Lynne and Roberta are with us when the transfers are announced. We organise a tally and pretty soon we realise that we've probably done it: enough votes for a quarter of the quota, the magic figure. Neil is madly scribbling – my affectionate term for tallying since I can't do it – and smiling and yes, it's enough and I'm over the line to get the deposit back. We let head office know and people are delighted. Of course I'm eliminated and my campaign is over now but with nearly 32,000 votes it is a cause to smile. We cheer and clap and I walk away feeling good. It's also good to discover that when I am eliminated I pass 10,000 votes to Marian Harkin. It's time for the mad mirrors again, time to celebrate our achievement and the end of Libertas. We stay up late. We really have earned this drink and we are all happy to eke out the last of the campaign. When I get up in the morning, I will no longer be the candidate.

Tuesday 9 June

It's so strange. All that madness and running round just stopped. The phone rings and it's *The Tubridy Show* to know if I want to come on tomorrow with some other first-time candidates and talk about the experience. I agree. Mags and I pack our bags, which seem to have grown in the past few days, and finally drag them all out to the van. The sun is shining and it's odd to see the posters on the road back to Sligo, looking suddenly out of place, plain wrong, now that there is no campaign. It's funny too to think I can go into a shop or walk up a street now just because I fancy doing it, not because I need to. As we drive up the hill to our house, there's a really touching moment: some of my posters are tied to trees with a sign attached to them that says, 'Well done, Susan. We're proud of you.' It brings a tear and when I get home, it's to find it was my neighbours, Fabian and Catherine and their family, who were so thoughtful.

Now all the stuff out of the car – the detritus of the campaign; newspapers, apples, tissues, badges and stickers. There's the Lisbon treaty document I couldn't find last week and there's Sabina's warm rug. I know it's time to end but it will be hard to stop and make the world revolve at a more sedate speed again. Hugs for M. I can't quite hug the van so instead take that photo – of me with the back window down! And off they go – the Labour Party, the campaign and the candidate. Just a little over ten weeks since I joined the Party and was unveiled. Now I really understand the meaning of the word 'whirlwind'.

Wednesday 10 June
The Tubridy Show bright and early. It goes well but when we are asked if we would do it all again, one says definitely not. I say I really enjoyed it and I will talk to the party about what happens next but that I have made no decision. My piece appears in the *Mail* and I am happy with it. Other people who read it say they enjoyed it.

Thursday 11 June

On my way to Leinster House, I bump into FF minister of state Martin Mansergh outside the Department of Agriculture. We shake hands and he congratulates me and says, smiling, that Charles Haughey stood four times before he got elected! I'm not sure I welcome the name-check. Then I bump into one of my contacts for that famous *World in Action* – a man I literally haven't seen for eighteen years. It's not often someone gets to say, 'Thank you for offering to go to jail rather than revealing my identity.' A friend rings to tease and say that I have obviously been 'bitten by the bug', if what I said on RTÉ yesterday was true. It's an expression I hadn't ever heard used in this context but oh, my goodness, do I hear it a lot now.

Sunday 14 June

I go to the Labour Party's thank-you to the candidates and the elected, in the Button Factory in Temple Bar. There's a big crowd and the sun is shining. The media are there and we have photos and Eamon does an interview. In his usual generous way, Proinsias stands back to allow me to stand next to Eamon for the photos and TV. I smile to myself as I realise there was a time when I didn't know any of that who stands where stuff. The three MEPs, the North-West Euro candidate and the Dublin by-election candidates troop on to the stage and we get a big round of applause. Joan Burton and Eamon make speeches of thanks and praise and there is a funny short film of all the campaigns. Even my little red dress makes an appearance. We adjourn for a drink and a chat, then we say our goodbyes. It's been a week of goodbyes: it's necessary, I think, to withdraw in phases and to have the chance to thank all the people in the party who helped behind the scenes in many different ways.

It was a successful election for the Labour Party. A total of a hundred and thirty two councillors elected. The party now has more councillors in Dublin than Fianna Fáil. Three MEPs were elected, an enormous achievement, and Eamon Gilmore has continued to hold his position in the polls as the country's most popular leader.

What I Have Learned

I met the good, the bad and the downright ugly – politicians that is – and I've shaken hands with all of them. You have to; it's part of the unwritten rule of making sure that in public, it's all smiles and handshakes even when the wheels are falling off or your political enemy is sitting next to you. It would be unbearable if basic courtesies were not observed and in truth we can, at moments, put aside our politics and enjoy observations from the same standpoint.

To survive in politics you need a warm smile, a firm handshake and a thick neck. And a good head for names! Once you put yourself in the public domain, you are fair game for insults, criticisms, compliments and observations, and if you're a woman, these will extend to how you look and what you wear. Total strangers will use the ease and anonymity of email to slag you off much more readily than people will write to say good things. Indeed, they may even say it to your face. Your best response is a smile. It's a smile game.

It's a me, myself, I, game too – *mé féinism* – and if you can't play that game, don't get in the ring. As one adviser put it: every dog sucks his own paw. It's very true. Every day is another opportunity to improve 'the profile', to be 'out there', to be 'in the public eye'. Maximising the profile is the driver of much local activity. Those in politics live and breathe in the goldfish bowl of self-publicity until they are confident of their own position or have sufficient power. Then they can afford to think more about the 'common good' – of the party or of the country. Many never do either.

Politics are local – right down to the street, townland or neighbourhood. Irish people remain very connected to their politicians and want to know that they will be 'looked after': even if they never actually ask their politician for help, they like to believe that they could do so. This could be rechristened 'doing a Haughey': many constituents defended Charles Haughey to the bitter end: they got what they needed and would not say a bad word about him. Haughey played the game to perfection and his private wealth, golden circles and Charvet shirts never bothered many of his voters because he never bit the hand that kept him in Dáil Éireann.

In many ways, our politics are too local. Even MEPs and TDs will be asked about potholes and decrepit schools. Yes, they should know about their constituency, but councillors should be the real powerhouses at local level, leaving TDs and MEPs to try to see the bigger picture for the constituency, the country and the EU. How can the level of debate, of opposition, of rigour in the Dáil about how to run the country be of a good standard when TDs have lists of fallen trees and housing requests to attend to? Vesting more power at local level is a very hot potato and there are many in Dáil Éireann who would fight tooth and nail to stop that devolution of power and influence; they see such a development as a threat rather than an opportunity.

Politics is hard work too. Having the electorate as your ultimate employer means you have to keep in touch and stay close:

the vicious circle of 'keeping the profile' never ends. Do your shopping right across the constituency, so that even buying the family groceries becomes an act of political engagement! There is no escape. Voters feel they own you and to a certain extent and that's true – their vote is their expression of faith in you and it's the biggest expression of faith they can make. Having made it, they will stop you on the street and ask for advice or help, call you or mail you. How to say no? You can't really, if you're doing the job properly. Voters often test their politicians by writing or contacting several representatives with a query or request and waiting to see who replies and gets the job done. It's no bad test.

I am struck by the amount of talking that's done; I think it outweighs the action quite significantly. Does that mean you have to go every funeral in the constituency? Well, not as an MEP – not in the North-West anyway – but rural TDs do their fair share of grieving; it's a way of keeping in touch and of showing a more caring side. Have no doubt that the less scrupulous ones will be all the more scrupulous about attending funerals.

I learned that people like to talk and like you to listen, that if you smile, they will smile back and that by and large, voters are polite and respectful, even if they disagree with your politics. And proportional representation gives people the chance to say, 'I'll look after you,' – and they mean it. A Number 13 is a preference; it's just not quite as useful as a Number 1!

I believe that, for many people, politics is football. Even when the team on the pitch is unfit, not working together and couldn't score a point to save their lives, it's still *your* team and you go on supporting them through thick, thin and even thinner. This atavistic loyalty which brooks no argument will remain a part of political life in Ireland even if we manage to throw off the genetic imprint of the Civil War.

There is a new Ireland out there, not yet quite engaged with our political system, not quite engaged with our mindset but slowly growing in numbers – significant enough to class us as multicultural. In time this group will raise its voice and change the tone and manner of our politics. If this led to the end of stroke politics and *mé féinism*, it would be welcome indeed.

The cliché that our political system has many failings means different things to different people. The biggest failing, I found, was that politics remains, by and large, the preserve of those with enough money to fund their own campaigns. Those with access to cash have leverage in their party and in an election because the plain and simple fact is that it costs money to campaign and campaigning is becoming more expensive. Those at the bottom of the financial pile rarely make it into the arena, no matter how great their talents or experience. This *is* a flaw.

I found too that there are many decent politicians who care about what they do and who work hard to try to make a difference. Very often it is the quiet TDs and councillors who don't bother with the whirl of publicity, preferring to pound the streets and shift the pile of requests and problems and get answers for those who can't do it for themselves.

Like any homogeneous grouping, politicians are anything but. All sorts are there, although statistically still far too few women – but there is one thing they all have in common. They are willing to put themselves through the physical and emotional rigours of an election campaign. That trait alone sets them apart! Or should I say – us…